Confessing Christ and Doing Politics

James W. Skillen
Editor

Essays by

Senator Mark O. Hatfield
Joel Nederhood
Gordon Spykman
Bernard Zylstra
Rockne McCarthy
James Skillen

Association for Public Justice Education Fund
Box 56348, Washington, D.C. 20011

© Association for Public Justice Education Fund, 1982.

Published by the Association for Public Justice Education Fund, Box 56348, Washington, D.C. 20011. No part of this book may be reproduced and distributed without obtaining the prior permission of the publisher.   Printed in Canada.

Library of Congress Cataloging in Publication Data

Skillen, James W., editor
    Confessing Christ and Doing Politics.
Washington, D.C.: Association for Public Justice
                    Education Fund

103 pages
8203   811110   Preassigned Card No.: 81-71233

ISBN: 0-936456-02-7

Cover design by Norm Matheis.

Contents

Acknowledgments

A book composed of several essays requires the cooperation of each author who must be willing to submit to the
discipline of a larger editorial design. The Editor wishes to
thank each of the authors for his fine spirit in this regard.
Furthermore, we must thank the many members of the
APJ Education Fund's conference planning committees
who did the hard work of organizing major international
Christian political conferences between 1977 and 1980.
Those conferences were the occasions when five of the
following essays were first presented. Finally, sincere
thanks to John and Susan Skillen for their editorial and
typing services in preparing the final draft of this book.

Introduction

Jesus said to His disciples, "apart from me you can do nothing" (John 15:5). Despite that strong statement, Christians have attempted all kinds of actions apart from Christ. Politics is one area of life where Christians have frequently sought a basis for action outside the "restrictions" of the Christian confession. Yet many Christians realize that Christ's claim of total lordship over life cannot be dismissed.

The following essays explore the connection between confessing Christ and doing politics. If we can do nothing apart from Christ, then how should we live politically? In particular, how should we *American* Christians face up to our contemporary political responsibilities? Although a new vitality among Christians is on display in the political arena today, the question about how politics relates to the Christian confession has not yet been answered to the satisfaction of all.

Recently, for example, Jerry Falwell, President of the Moral Majority, stated clearly that "Moral Majority is not a religious organization; it's political. There is no theological agreement in Moral Majority." (*Christianity Today*, September 4, 1981). Moral Majority is a relatively new political organization on the American scene that is usually identified with Christian fundamentalism or the

"Christian right." Yet it is clear from Falwell's statement that the Christian confession is not definitive for Moral Majority. The question remains: How shall confessing Christians take their stand in politics?

Most of the essays in this book originated in the circles of the Association for Public Justice and the APJ Education Fund. Five of them were presented as addresses at the international political conferences sponsored by the APJ Education Fund. Senator Mark Hatfield (R. Oregon) was the keynote speaker at the first conference in 1977 when he urged Christians to stand firmly in Christ in order to render justice to every neighbor. He rejected the idea that Christian politics is merely successful power politics; instead, he affirmed the biblical call to *service*.

Joel Nederhood, a minister-evangelist who addressed another of the political conferences, knows all too well that few Christians see a clear connection between the confession of Christ and their political lives. The problem, he points out, is a competing religion—an American civil religion—that gets in the way of authentic biblical Christianity.

Gordon Spykman sounds a note that has characterized APJ from the start, namely, that politics is action and not just words. A college theology professor who has served on the APJ Board, Spykman knows how dangerous empty words can be. It is not enough for Christians to learn how to use all the correct words for confessing Christ but to remain fruitless. The admonition from Jesus in John 15 explains that the branches of the vine which bear no fruit will be pruned away.

The first three essays call Christians to a distinctive, biblically obedient kind of political action—the action of service rooted without apology in Christ.

Part II explores the context of a distinctively Christian approach to politics in our day by trying to answer some pressing questions. What does the Bible say? What is justice? What is the state? Must Christians be tolerant of everyone? What about tolerance of evil? What is the character of American civil religion? How should our

6

earthly political actions be conditioned or affected by confidence in the coming of God's Kingdom?

Bernard Zylstra wrote an essay some years ago that remains helpful in clarifying the meaning of Christian political involvement. Zylstra is a political theorist who has been close to Christian political efforts in Europe, Canada, and the United States for years. He is a Research Associate of the APJ Education Fund, and we appreciate his willingness to let us use an edited version of his essay. He argues persuasively that the connection between the Bible and politics, between confessing Christ and living responsibly in a modern state, is the norm of *justice*.

Rockne McCarthy explores in more detail the meaning of civil religion in America, showing not only how it functions in the hearts of people but how it structures the political system itself. McCarthy is a professor of American history and politics who has served almost from the beginning of APJ's existence as a member of its Board and staff.

James Skillen's essays reflect a concern with two particular problems confronting Christians in the political arena—tolerance and the future. Can tolerance be a genuine ingredient in Christian politics? Aren't Christians supposed to fight against every kind of evil and try to enforce righteousness in the nation? Should the confession of Christ lead to tolerance and public pluralism or to intolerance and conformity? With regard to the future we face another series of questions. Should we Christians think of ourselves as sojourners passing through this world to the next? Or should we adopt the attitude of homesteaders and householders who take this world seriously, situating ourselves firmly in the here and now? Toward what end are we moving? What does Christ's future return have to do with the present practice of politics?

We hope that these essays will help to lay a firmer foundation for Christian political responsibility in the years ahead. As an association of Christians whose aim is to nurture responsible citizenship, the Association for Public

Justice urges Christians to think deeply about the implications of the Christian confession for political life—not to think without acting, but to meditate and debate seriously in the midst of political action.

The APJ Education Fund seeks to encourage this process of reflection, debate, and discussion. It is an educational and research organization working to provide perspective on public life from a biblical point of view. Through its basic research, policy analysis, and publications it provides service to associations such as APJ. The APJ Education Fund's first book, a study guide entitled, *Christians Organizing for Political Service*, can help to structure group discussion in which the themes and essays of this book can be fruitfully debated in a small group setting.

Jesus did not tell His disciples *only* that they could do nothing apart from Him. Chapter 15 of John's Gospel presents a picture of the fruitful vineyard and the caring gardener. Jesus explained that He is the vine, His Father the gardener, and His followers the branches of the vine. His promise is that if a person "remains in me and I in him, he will bear much fruit." We live by faith in Christ, our vine, and we have every reason to believe that our political lives can be fruitful for His sake and our neighbor's sake if we are faithful to Jesus and His Father, our Father.

Part I
THE CALL TO ACTION

1

Christ's Call to Service

Senator Mark O. Hatfield

I have sensed for many years that we in the North American evangelical community have had a burning question put to us, both from within our community and from outside as well. What do we do with our political responsibility? Many have felt that political activity is beyond the scope of appropriate Christian involvement. I have frequently been asked by other Christians how I could retain my faith and still be a politician. There has been a general tendency to believe that faith is non-political and that the two realms are totally incompatible.

But today among the same circles there is a growing consensus, a reawakening perhaps, that Christian political and social involvement should be a part of our natural witness. This new awareness of the integration of our faith with our political, economic, and social life is helping us to recover the wholeness of the biblical message.

Mark O. Hatfield is a Republican Senator from Oregon. A frequent speaker and author of many articles, he has written *Conflict and Conscience* (Waco, TX: Word Books, 1971), and *Between a Rock and a Hard Place* (Waco, TX: Word Books, 1976).

The further question remains, however, of how, exactly, that Christian responsibility is to be exercised. What should be the shape of the Christian witness to the state? On this issue, a variety of views are being explored, tested, and debated, both theologically and practically. On the one hand, very conservative Christian political activists speak of turning the nation back to God by increasing America's wealth, power, and prestige in order to defeat our foes. On the other hand, the left-wing activists are willing to go to jail for pouring blood on the Pentagon steps. Some might deny that one extreme or the other is actually Christian. For our present purposes, we may ascribe righteousness as far as motives are concerned to the entire spectrum of action. The method, the shape, the scope, and the purpose of Christian political activity is the issue demanding our attention.

Let us consider some of the options open to us, not necessarily expecting to achieve unity and agreement, but in order to shed light upon our pilgrimage as believers. Since the time of Constantine, when Christianity became the official religion of the establishment, Christians have struggled with this very vexing problem. How could they both carry out the responsibilities of governing the state and reconcile those actions with the teaching of the gospel of Jesus Christ?

The answer to this question in the medieval period was straightforward. The state was to operate according to the principle of retribution—the *lex talionis:* an eye for an eye, a tooth for a tooth—in order to serve its divinely appointed function. Those whose vocation during this time was to carry out that function, from the kings who ruled by divine right to the soldiers who fought their battles, were to do so dutifully and devoutly. But those others who were called to specifically religious vocations could pay more serious attention to Christ's gospel of forgiving love and contemplate living like Him. Saintly perfection was a possibility for them.

The Reformation, however, brought changes in the way Christians considered these issues. Luther and his

12

followers rejected the notion that some are meant to be saintly, like the monks, while others could live a less holy existence. Luther declared that each person in every walk of life should try to follow Christ's pattern in his individual relationships with others. But when people operate at the level of the responsibility for society at large, or corporately, then they are to follow a different standard, that of retributive justice. The state was seen as an order of creation, as Luther called it. The way it operated was part of God's design.

The Calvinist view, according to my understanding, differed from the Lutheran by stating that the standards which govern the state cannot be known naturally, but come from the revelation of the Bible. Nor does Calvinism accept a dualism of principles for the behavior of Christians, one for personal relationships and one for civil power. One set of norms ought to govern the personal and public lives of all people, including non-believers. Those norms are something more than simply the justice of an eye for an eye, but something less than agape love. A holy commonwealth, a type of theocracy, is found in the Calvinist model.

After the turn of the present century, a Christian pacifist view more visibly entered the American picture. With historical roots at least as deep as Calvinism, this view holds that the standard for both the individual and the state is forgiving, agape love. Both individuals and the state, and both believers and non-believers, can and should act according to that norm. But with the coming of World War II, support for the liberal pacifist view was severely shaken.

More pragmatic views of Christian political responsibility emerged, perhaps the foremost of which was the theological realism of Reinhold Niebuhr. He combined certain elements of each of the earlier perspectives, believing that there was always hope for a little more relative justice than presently existed. But the reality of sin must temper our optimism and sense of achievement.

Nearly all of these views, inadequately outlined here, to

13

be sure, have one element in common. They assume that Christians who have social and political responsibility will be required to do things which would let the agape love of Christ serve as the basis for their public actions. Furthermore, all these views since the time of Constantine tend to assume that political actions and responsibilities show the difference in values between those who have faith in a living God and those who do not. Yet, if we are realistic, we realize that for much of contemporary society the standards of Christian love are irrelevant. There is no commitment to live with Christ as Lord. He is not even an ideal to be followed.

Thus, we must consider a view of Christian political witness which assumes that there will be a difference between those whose lives are based on faith in Jesus Christ as Lord and Savior, and those for whom such faith is simply not a factor. In other words, our Christian stance toward the state should be based on the recognition that the church universal has an identity and an ethic distinct from society in general. In this view, of course, there is the implicit temptation for Christians to see themselves as a pure and holy band of people withdrawn from the world while regarding the rest of society as damned. Such an attitude of withdrawal can easily lead to the fallacy that no political witness is really necessary or even possible. In so doing, the fact of Christ's lordship over all the world is ignored, and thus denied. Nevertheless, if we guard against the danger of conceding the world to the devil, I believe it is possible to construct a creative and vital model for a Christian's political witness.

This witness, as I see it, must begin with the fact that the Christian is called to live according to a kingdom whose reign and reality has not yet been accepted by society at large. The heart of our political witness must be rooted in our faithfulness to the kingdom proclaimed by our Lord. The vision of that kingdom places us at odds with the prevailing values of our society.

Let us look at the message of Jesus to His time and to

ours. The gospel accounts reveal Christ's persistent exposure of the shortcomings of the prevailing systems of His day. His call to discipleship beckoned those who followed to begin a new life, both personally and corporately, on new foundations. For Christ, the problems of injustice and the lack of social righteousness were at the very heart of the problem. The values upon which the existing institutions and political movements were based were the desire for power and domination, the quest for money, and the lure of prestige and recognition. The kingdom of Christ, on the other hand, proclaimed a new life based not on the values of selfishness but on a radical selflessness. The false values of money, glory, and power are to be forsaken. Instead of hoarding, there is to be sharing. Instead of ambition and glory, humility is to reign. Instead of power and domination, there is to be voluntary service.

The values of Christ's kingdom are as shockingly revolutionary in our own modern technological society as they were to the provincial Palestine or the militarist Roman Empire of His own day. Giving oneself to Christ and His society means that one's life will be utterly revolutionized. This is why I believe that one does not find in Christ's life an endorsement of any of the political trends of His day, be they the crusades of the Zealots, the approach of the Sadducees to work with the present system, or the haughty legalistic attempt of many of the Pharisees to achieve religious purity. Christ invites us to follow Him in creating a new life and a new society.

We must not suppose that Christ was a-political. On the contrary, His message could not have been addressed more pointedly to the social and political injustices and realities of His time. The Sermon on the Mount, for instance, contains four beatitudes which deal with giving comfort and hope to the oppressed, and four others which give encouragement and blessing to those who help the cause of the oppressed. The truth is that our Lord set forth a hope for social and political renewal, for achieving God's purposes and standards of justice, which was far more radical in its dimensions than any of the movements of His time.

That hope is rooted in a response to the good news of the kingdom of God, and involves, today as then, a total transformation of the way life is defined.

In the light of this gospel of the kingdom, let us look briefly at the church as the basis of political witness to our society. I believe that the existence and the very life of the church must be at the heart of our Christian witness to the state. Christ's own images for the presence of His disciples in society—light, leaven, salt—all suggest that those called to God's purposes will have a distinctive identity, a unique character. The quality of this presence in the world is to be a sign of the kingdom's promise, and thus it is to shed light, to add a distinctive flavor, and to enable extraordinary hope and possibilities for the world.

Our problem, perhaps, has been that the church has not shed light because its own light has been too engulfed in darkness; it has not been the salt of the world because its own life has lost its savor; it cannot be the leaven because its own life is lacking the energy of God's Spirit. Given the great numbers of people represented by the church today, the sophisticated technology available to us, the friendly, or at worst indifferent, environment in which the church in North America exists, the church's lack of influence in the world may indeed appear as a discouraging contrast to the bold and dynamic witness of the early church, planted as it was in a pagan society with but a handful of people, few of whom were well-educated, well-bred, or influential.

Our Christian witness to the state must begin by re-establishing, in our own life as God's people, that quality which gives genuine witness to the kingdom. Our standard is never one of withdrawal, but rather one of pointed, courageous, and sacrificial interest and penetration into all passages of the world. Through the record of biblical history, God has worked to achieve His purposes for all the world by calling out a people to be faithful to Him, and then calling them to pour out their lives for the purposes of God's justice, of His love for all of humanity. Our task is always to call society toward the kingdom. We must never suppose that our only responsibility is to get individual

16

people saved. Rather, we must continually hold forth the messages and the promises of the kingdom of God to a secular society, to a society that does not yet proclaim Christ's lordship.

Of course if one temptation is to withdraw from the world, the opposite one is to take part in the world's systems uncritically, playing by their rules, their standards, in order to work for God's purposes. Again the Bible gives us, I believe, a different word of counsel. We are to be in the world, because Christ is Lord over all, but that is not to be mistaken for being like the world, captive ourselves to its myths, idols, and gods, absorbed by its system of thought, power, and life. Our fundamental allegiance and loyalty is always to another kingdom. Hence we can expect a tension, a clash, between the calling of that kingdom and those purposes to which societies and nations want to give themselves. Not to expect such a confrontation is to believe that the kingdom has already arrived and to nullify the witness and presence our life is intended to bear.

We must always ask society to embrace some aspect of the kingdom vision beyond society's present reality. Thus our presence and our witness will always have a prophetic quality. This is true by definition, simply because the kingdom has not yet been fulfilled. Our words and our witness must be translated into partial goals and be addressed to contemporary issues, such as the goals of human rights, or equality, or the elimination of poverty, or a new international economic order of justice and disarmament.

For instance, during recent months of my work as a senator (1976-1977), I have been involved in trying to take tobacco out of the Food for Peace program, to stop the funding for the neutron bomb, to combat congressional attempts to deny funds for President Carter's pardon program for draft evaders, to establish a world peace tax fund. Although at first glance there seems to be little uniformity or pattern in these activities, in each case my Christian commitment was fundamental to my motivations. I of course disavow any pretense of knowing a definitive Christian position on such miscellaneous issues, and in the legislating arena these questions were debated in secular terms. Yet in each case an element of judgment was brought to bear on present policies, goals, attitudes, values, assumptions; a stance of challenging policies rather than accepting the general drift of things. As it happens, each of these proposals was defeated. Yet in each case, a witness was borne, I trust, to the goals which would move us in the direction of the kingdom, as I understand it. Essential to all of these is a prophetic stance which always begins at the point of what the kingdom asks of us all.

We of course know that sin will pose obstacles to the full achievement of these goals, and we know that even if and when they are achieved, the call of the kingdom still beckons us. We know too that even these goals cannot be reached without some fundamental changes in the values of materialism, pride, and power. Yet I believe that we can and must address a witness to the state which entails both judgment and hope. The judgment: that its present course is headed on the path to destruction and despair. The hope: that a vision of life exists, and that even the smallest steps taken toward it are better than treading the present path, broad and smooth as it may seem. If the challenge seems great, we might remember the simple yet compelling way in which an Old Testament prophet describes our responsibility in society: "He has showed you, O man, what is good; and what does the Lord require of you, but to do justice, to love kindness, and to walk humbly with your God" (Micah 6:8, *RSV*).

2

God's Will and America's Destiny

Joel Nederhood

One speaks of America's destiny against a background of a long tradition of people who have encouraged one another by saying: "America is indeed the greatest nation in the world, the nation that God is going to use to establish His purposes in creation." European explorers and settlers as early as Columbus himself thought about the New World in terms of God's great purposes for mankind. Many of our colonial ancestors came to America with a sense that God was bringing them here not only to do something for themselves, but to do something for all people everywhere. By the time of the Revolutionary War many people were already speaking about America's special destiny. Henry Wadsworth Longfellow gave voice in the nineteenth century to a common and popular senti-ment when he wrote:

> Thou, too sail on! O Ship of State,
> Sail on! O Union, strong and great.
> Humanity with all its fears,

Joel Nederhood is Minister of *The Back to God Hour*, interna-tional broadcast of the Christian Reformed Church.

> With all its hopes for future years,
> Is hanging breathless on thy fate.

Herman Melville presents an even more religious statement of that early vision of America's destiny in his novel *Whitejacket:*

> God has predestined, mankind expects great things for our race, and great things we feel in our souls. We are the pioneers of the world, the advance guard sent through the wilderness of untried things to break a new path in the new world that is ours. Long enough have we debated whether indeed the political messiah has come, but he has come in us. And let us remember that with ourselves almost for the first time in history national selfishness is unbounded philanthropy. But we cannot do a good to America, but we give alms to the world.

This vision of a land with a special gift to give to all the nations has been nurtured within the bosom of our country.

This sense of having a special destiny is an important element of what can be called the American "civil religion." Sociologists and anthropologists have come to the conclusion that all cultures are held together by a kind of religious cohesion, by certain basic beliefs, which, citing Eric Voegelin's definition, form a sort of "obligatory minimum dogma or enforced basic consensus" for the maintaining of a political society. These constitute a "civil religion." Those today who associate patriotism and religious fervor appeal to the overtly religious framework in which the founding fathers stated the principles of the American Republic. But even those today for whom the political society of America has become totally secularized still assume certain dogmas of America's civil religion such as the belief that political sovereignty rests with the people and that the majority should rule. Crossing as it does the political spectrum, this sense of America's destiny, described with religious fervor throughout our nation's history, announced that this land is God's gift to the world.

If, however, we take a second look in the light of God's Word at this traditional view of the destiny of America, we discover that it contains elements which are unchristian, if not anti-christian. Herman Melville's description of America as the new and great political messiah which God has brought into the world should make us shudder. The civil religion that has developed in the U.S.A. is not really supernatural, but is in fact a natural entity, a natural phenomenon found in all the nations of the world. Inasmuch as "Religion USA" seeks to equate and identify the destiny of America with the will of God Almighty, it is essentially pagan. Such a vision can keep us from recognizing, confessing, and changing the sinful injustices against the poor, the unborn, the oppressed of every kind, injustices which deform the face of America. Moreover, a sense of destiny that divorces the benefits of civil religion from the requirements of God's righteous sovereignty is often promoted by the very educational system which supposes its own religious neutrality. By law, ordinary education has been separated in this country from the testimony of the Word of the living God.

We must recognize, however, that the problem with America cannot be described in terms of certain discrete evils to which we might point. The problem within America lies rather in the fact that there is something wrong at the very root of its poltical system. The problem is not just with one party or another, or with the way both parties function together. Something has gone awry within our political system itself. In fact, by enacting the near deification of the population and the rule of the majority, our political system is more an expression of the rationalistic Enlightenment than of the Christian gospel. For this reason we have not really had justice and equity within our nation. When we look at our government, we find in many instances nothing more than an institutionalization of selfishness and special interests. We must ask ourselves whether something is radically wrong with the very structure of American political life.

A renewed and responsible call for public justice must

21

arise, not because of an evil here and an evil somewhere else, but from a clear understanding of the nature of state and government, and from a keen perception of the fact that state and government can function properly only beneath the rule of the Lord Jesus Christ. Recognizing the evil that exists in our country today and the non-christian elements in the structure of our national life, we reluctantly come to the conclusion that idols are at work within our land. We might turn to Psalm 96 for an expression of the mighty contrast that runs through the entire Old Testament and reappears in the New, the contrast between what it means to live beneath the rule of God and what it means to live beneath the rule of the idols. "All the gods of the peoples are idols; but the Lord made the heavens . . . Say among the nations, 'the Lord reigns!' " Of course at the time Psalm 96 was written, the idols were represented by figures that could be stood in the corner or placed in a temple. Today our idols are the great secular gods upon which we depend for our defense, our welfare, our education, our economic prosperity.

Hence, when as Christian people we think about the destiny of America, we must first dissociate ourselves from an easy identification of the Christian cause with the cause of the United States of America. Nevertheless, having recognized that some things about the very structure of our country are radically wrong, we must also recognize that we have great responsibilities for the United States. We as the people of God cannot simply stand back and wring our hands and cry out in despair. Rather, God is calling us to participate fully in the life of this land in order to bring into the national experience the reality of repentance and turning, making possible a day when justice shall flow down like the mighty waters of the sea over our nation and God will be glorified within its borders. Although America itself is certainly not the bearer of God's redeeming grace for the world, it is still true that no other nation is quite like ours. We may indeed be grateful that in the good providence of God we are citizens of America. We are

American Christians, and can look at our land and rejoice in it. In spite of all the strange rhetoric that people have used to describe our past, it seems to me to be true that America, in spite of itself, does reflect certain elements of the Christian world-view that are actual and magnificent. Scholars such as Arendt Th. Van Leeuwen have analyzed the impact of Christianity upon modern culture and demonstrated that in a very real sense the insights residing in the Christian faith gave birth to the advantages we enjoy now. Our economic prosperity, our cherished ideals of freedom, are not the results solely of an Enlightenment concept of social contracts among property owners.

In some strange and marvelous way that concept of freedom operates here in the United States of America. Each of us is free to be a Christian. Every mature adult in the United States, of whatever race or background, is free to vote. We have the right to form voluntary associations. We are free to form religious associations. We can form voluntary political associations, even for the purpose of bringing pressure to bear on the very government that permits their existence. We who use broadcasting benefit especially from the glorious freedom we do have in this country. The fact that we can actually take our world-and-life view and air it across the land spells freedom. *The Back to God Hour* has been built over the years on the understanding that it is necessary to bring to our American nation a Christian world-and-life view, and we can do that continuously. We are free to elect Christian men and women to offices on various levels, who can take on themselves the responsibility to represent in the high eschelons of government not only their constituency but also their Lord. All of this is why we as American Christians cannot simply stand back and wring our hands. We cannot stand back and observe America from a distance; we are people who are part of America.

In this country where there is so much freedom, God has placed many people like us. Why did He place us here? I believe that God has called us to be His ambassadors not only to bring the gospel of salvation in Christ to the in-

23

dividuals of this nation, but to bring reformation and renewal to the United States of America through the gospel of Christ's kingdom. Perhaps such a task sounds too difficult, too unrealistic. Is there really any hope that people like us can be used by God to turn our country around? I believe that there is.

I believe that the keys to bringing reformation to America are threefold: our *faith* in Christ, our *vision* of His kingdom, and our godly *fear*.

We will be able to bring about change in our land only if we are a people whose hearts are filled with *faith*, faith in the Lord Jesus Christ and faith in the Scriptures that serve as the link between us and our Savior. The Bible provides the truth and wisdom that enable us to see not only our salvation but the implications of our salvation for all of life. Political activity, just as action in any sphere of life, will be worth nothing at all unless our lives are anchored completely in the Scripture and the vision it provides. I might again refer to Psalm 96 as one of the many parts of the Bible that set up the fundamental contrast mentioned earlier: the contrast between the worship of God and obedience to Him, and the worship of idols and obedience to them. That contrast is built upon the fundamental fact that all of life is religion and all human action is religious. What we do in factories, what we do in our kitchens, what we do in our bedrooms, what we do everywhere somehow reflects our understanding of the God whom we seek to serve. This vision of life is itself kept alive only by living every single day out of the Word of the living God.

Many people today of course talk about Jesus, about His lordship, and they say all kinds of nice things about Jesus. Yet too often the Jesus about whom they talk is basically a figment of their imaginations. The Jesus whom we serve in our political life must be the Jesus who meets us on the pages of the Bible. We as Christians must make sure that our plans for political action, our ideas of political effectiveness and political results, are based four-square on whether or not we are people of the Book, on whether or not we are people who have bound our lives one hundred percent to that special revelation that God has given us. For it is by that Word that our actions will be judged. In prayerful humility, we must confess that whatever we may accomplish will be dependent upon the living God of heaven and earth, who with His Spirit brings us into His service and makes us His children. Everything depends on faith, but if our faith is real and if it is biblical through and through, I believe that God can use us to change our land.

What *vision* is borne by our faith? It is not a vision of what *we're* going to accomplish or of what God might use *us* to perform that should form the basis of our action. The basis of our action is rather the vision we receive from the Scripture of a new world built on the finished work of the Lord Jesus Christ. It is the vision of Jesus who, when He was about to ascend into heaven, said, "All authority in heaven and on earth has been given to me." The authority of Jesus must be proclaimed within our world by ministers. But the reign of Christ, the rule of His kingdom, must also be expressed by fathers and mothers, by business people, by believers in all areas of life. The authority of Jesus must be expressed in the political arena too, by men and women who have subjected themselves to the rule of Christ and who understand clearly that Jesus wants to see the monument of justice erected everywhere. This is our vision: the vision of the triumph of God. This is our prayer: "Thy will be done on earth as it is in heaven." By this petition, states the Heidelberg Catechism, we pray that men and women everywhere may discharge their offices and their callings in terms of the will of God. I believe that with this vision, God can use us.

But to be used, we must also have the *fear* of the Lord. Our fear of the Lord arises from a sense of God's righteous judgment in store for our nation if our vision is not fulfilled. The twentieth chapter of Ezekiel, for instance, tells what happens to a country that serves idols instead of serving the Lord God of heaven and earth.

> Moreover, I gave them the statutes that were not good and ordinances by which they could not have life; and I defiled them through their very gifts in making them offer by fire all their first-born, that I might horrify them; I did it that they might know that I am the Lord (20:25-26, RSV).

When we speak about the judgment of God, we tend to imagine fire and brimstone, thunder and lightning, and things like that. But as the prophets show, the judgment of God can fall upon a nation in ways more subtle and more severe. The very laws of a nation may bring death instead of life, cursing instead of blessedness. Some people may believe America today to be perilously near such a condition.

The hour is already late as we take up the task God gives us. Nevertheless, as we remind our fellow citizens of the judgment in store for nations who worship idols, we may be thankful that we do so not from prisons or in exile, not as dissidents or subversives. We can speak as full American citizens who have a joyful task, for the message that we bring is not only of judgment, but of hope, and our call is the call to life. As we take up our task, let us keep in mind these questions:

What about our faith? Is it really strong, strong enough to keep us fully committed to God's great Word?

What about our vision? Do we worship Jesus only as the One who can save us from the wrath to come, or do we really understand that Jesus is the One to whom all authority is given in heaven and on earth?

Are we people who have the fear of the Lord in our souls? Do we say with the apostle Paul, "Knowing the fear of the Lord, we persuade men"?

"Therefore, my beloved, be steadfast, immovable, always abounding in the work of the Lord, knowing that in the Lord your labor is not in vain" (I Cor. 15:58, *RSV*).

3

Beyond Words to Action

Gordon Spykman

Christians can be great organizers. We know how to organize homes, churches, schools, evangelistic campaigns, businesses, and countless other activities. Why then have we been unable to organize our efforts in the field of politics with the same success we have had in other areas of life? Why this blind spot? One of the principles of our faith is that Christ is Lord of all. All of life is to be submitted to His rule, and certainly life encompasses politics. And certainly politics is more than words. Research is essential, but it is not the goal in organizing Christian politics. Conferences, seminars, workshops, and publications must all be carried forward, but not as ends in themselves. Politics is action and action requires organizing. How do we get a handle on organizing Christian politics?

We may consider this problem of "organizing Christian politics" by looking at each word in turn. But since our

Gordon Spykman is Professor of Theology at Calvin College, Grand Rapids, Michigan. He is the author (with others) of *Society, State, and Schools* (Grand Rapids, MI: Eerdmans, 1981).

hesitancy and lack of success in organizing as Christians really begins with our reservations about politics itself, let's take the third word first and work backwards.

Are Christians still too isolationist with respect to the public sector of life? Do we hold our faith in one hand and politics in the other—as far apart as possible—trying to live in two different worlds? Or is it because we are still too individualistic, unable or unwilling to build Christian community together? Perhaps our problem with politics stems from divisions within the household of faith. For some of us, Christianity is primarily "sound doctrine." Doctrinalists locate the center of gravity for Christian living in the clear understanding of biblical truths, in the maintenance of doctrinal purity and orthodox faith. Others are "pietists" who stress sincere, heartfelt communion with God and the exercise of certain habits of devotion and personal conduct. Another group of Christians might be called the "worldviewers," those who are driven by an impulse to see what can be done to serve Christ's kingdom in all areas of life. Politics may be viewed so differently from these three pespectives that Christians cannot even find one another, much less organize together, in the political arena.

To approach this issue of "politics," we have to understand certain basic biblical guidelines, the first of which is that our whole life should be an exercise of Christian faith. What some Christians have called "the cultural mandate" holds for politics as well as for plowing the land, teaching a class, keeping house, doing business, building bridges, painting pictures, and whatever else we do. Politics too is part of the mandate which the Lord has laid upon us by virtue of creation. This is one of the guidelines, it seems to me, on which we ought to agree.

Secondly, we are called to live the life of faith in the midst of the world. Not on some isolated island, but at the crossroads of civilization where the Lord has placed us. The earth is the Lord's, not ours. And we must be active in it. Otherwise, how can we be salt or light?

The third biblical guideline is that our life in this world

28

should demonstrate something of the unity of life in Christ. We are the body of Jesus Christ, not separate members who have no relationship one to another. That unity is not constituted by sitting in the pew for an hour or two on Sunday. Christ did not say, "You are the lights of the world," but rather, "You are the *light*"—in the singular—like one mighty generating station. "You are the salt of the earth," not as tiny discrete grains, but *together* we are the salt. "You are a city built on a hill." A good city has a certain cohesion to it; it has an organization, a program, a policy, a constitution.

These are some of the guidelines provided by the Scriptures which must be kept clearly in mind if we are to honor our political calling. For politics too is an office which the Lord has entrusted to our care, an office as real as that of parent, or teacher, or preacher, or farmer. We must recognize that as *political* office its authority is God-given. Like all authority, it comes from above. Remember when Pilate asked the mute Jesus, "Won't you say anything? Don't you know I have the power, the authority to set you free or to keep you in bondage?" Jesus replied, "You would have no authority at all if it were not given to you from above" (John 19:10-11). That holds for every form of authority in life, including the authority which God has entrusted to us as Christian citizens. With that authority comes a certain responsibility or answerability. Authority always brings with it stewardship. As the Scriptures say, every steward is called, sooner or later, to give an account of his stewardship. So we are called to be guardians of the political authority which the Lord has entrusted to our care. Every kind of authority must be used for service. Political authority is perverted when placed in the service of interest-group or class struggles, which are as real in a capitalist as in a socialist society. Political authority exists for blessing, for service, for the exercise of justice that benefits others.

Next, what about the adjective "Christian" in this phrase, "organizing Christian politics"? Remember Abraham Kuyper's statement that "there is not a single square inch of the entire universe of which Christ does not say, 'This is mine.' " The Christian community should honor that claim and press it wherever possible. Christian politics is not to be understood, however, in the way that medieval Christians understood the *Corpus Christianum*. They believed that Christianity should be imposed, by force if necessary, upon all subjects of the realm. Many people still assume, mistakenly of course, that when Christians begin talking about Christian politics they want to recreate the medieval society.

A friend of mine, for instance, studying at Berkeley a dozen years ago during the height of the counter-culture "revolution," tells about a discussion of politics in which he became involved. Very quickly the others detected in his ideas a different perspective. They challenged him, "Who are you anyway?" "I'm a Christian," he replied. "A Christian! You Christians have had your chance since 313. Now it's our turn." They were referring to this long-lived assumption that society as a whole could be Christianized, and that Christianity could be imposed by the sword or by papal edict upon all people. That is not what we ought to mean by Christian politics.

Christian politics must respect the honest religious pluralism which is present in our society. The only sword at our disposal is the sword of the Spirit which is the persuasive power of God's Word. In this conviction we must go our way motivated by a sheer sense of obedience. We need not be success-oriented in the spirit of American jumbo politics, with its commitment to winning at all costs. Christians must seek the kind of political presence and voice and witness which finds its reason for existence not in its number of victories, but in its willingness to stand up and be counted. We must dare to be different, dare to work out an alternative, even while running the risk of being misunderstood and misrepresented.

Christian politics comes down to recognizing the totalitarian claim that Jesus made in those climactic words of Matthew's Gospel (Matt. 28:18-20), where he took the long series of great commissions he had been giving all

30

along and pulled them together in concentrated form. His final mandate to "go into all the world" is bigger than missions and evangelism. It also includes home life, school life, political life, all of life, as a redemptively updated restatement of the cultural mandate which the Father had given in the beginning. In so doing, Christ first laid upon us all his totalitarian claim, his unlimited claim to all authority. He then presented his unlimited challenge: "Go into all the world"—the world of the kitchen, of the academy, of downtown business, of law, of medicine, of politics—"teaching people to observe all that I have commanded." This unlimited task is backed up by Christ's promise of His unlimited presence: "Lo, I am with you always, even to the end of the world."

I have spoken briefly, first about *politics*, secondly about *Christian* politics. The verb in our phrase is the hardest of all to discuss: *organizing* Christian politics. Can the vision I have sketched—of a perspective on politics based on biblical principles and a biblical mandate—be organized?

Big claims are made these days for organization. One can claim too much for it, but one can also claim too little. The question of *how* to organize a movement is not actually the first question to be asked. The first question is, *what* to do? Then we must seek an organized way of doing it. The method must grow out of the message. The way one does it must somehow grow naturally out of what ought to be done. Methods of organizing things are not religiously neutral. They must be developed in ways that are consistent with the foundations upon which they are based. One of our difficulties, of course, in developing models for doing Christian politics is that we have no existing models on this continent to which we can point. Most Christians have never seen a Christian political model in operation, and therefore can hardly conceive of the possibility of working one out.

How one addresses the question of organized Christian politics depends on what one means by organization. If the idea of organization is limited exclusively to party formation, then I suspect we're not ready for organization. Perhaps we will never be ready for that. Perhaps we shouldn't even strive for the goal of a Christian party. It is possible that the party system as it has developed in the United States may be growing obsolete. It certainly seems to be moving into a phase of reduced importance. Organizing Christians does not necessarily mean entering the fray of American party politics as it now operates.

But if party politics need not determine the shape of our political action, what principles of political organization ought we to follow? Politics for many people means the hoopla of the election process itself: running candidates, campaigning, following results on television. But politics is more than elections. What is that "more"? Let me list a number of points, all reflecting a certain line of development, for further consideration.

1. We must focus once again on kingdom preaching. Something has to happen in the organized church if we are to be serious about organizing Christian politics. How can we as people of God be the salt of the world if the church as an institution has itself lost its salt? How can we be a leaven in the world if the church no longer carries the leaven within itself? How can we be a light out there if the light is dim inside? Something has to happen within the organized church if the stimulus to organize Christian politics is to flow from it. We must have our priorities straight in the pulpit and in the pew if we mean to move toward some form of creative and effective organized Christian politics.

2. Our Christian educational institutions must also keep clearly before them a biblical perspective on life. Too often we judge our success by enrollments or by coming out at year's end in the black. Sometimes we define the goals of Christian education in terms of self-perpetuation. In our educational institutions we need to open our eyes to the grand strategy of the kingdom, asking "Why are we teaching and in what direction are we seeking to move the younger generation?" Maybe it is time to develop a pool of financial resources so that we can take some of these

32

talented, dedicated young graduates and place them in strategic positions, economically, socially, politically, in our society where they can exercise their talents.

3. We will have to make the strongest possible pitch for the youth. I know that everybody else is pitching for them too. Every crosswind of contrary doctrine in our world is blowing their way. Their course of action, however, really comes down to choosing one of three alternatives. They may choose to go "secular," that is, to accept the state of affairs pretty much as it is and seek to accommodate themselves to it. Or they may choose to retreat, that is, to size up the world as evil and try to keep themselves uncontaminated by it. Or they may take the third avenue, a real alternative, and follow the Bible's strategy of reforming engagement in the world. I remember hearing Carl Henry say a few years ago that we've got to help our younger generation march under the banner of Jesus Christ or else assuredly they will be marching before long under other banners.

These basic ideas hold for the Christian community as a whole in the various dimensions of life. We must now go on to spell out more concretely our calling with respect to organized political action. Consider the following points:

1. We must support and sustain present organizations such as the Association for Public Justice, and await God's time. We must be alert to the time when God's people see the crucial nature of our cultural crises and sense, intuitively perhaps, the acute need for some sort of alternative. We must keep APJ alive so that we can be ready to serve when such a time comes. In the meantime, we continue to knock at the doors of the Christian community to let them know we are still here.

2. For the time being, organized Christian politics will have to continue, as APJ is doing, to develop issues around which to rally the principled commitment of the Christian community. We must find ways of structuring our leadership, perhaps by setting up research centers, certainly by encouraging a new climate of commitment and reflection within the Christian community. As a prere-

33

quisite for explicit forms of organization, we must continue both to articulate biblical principles and to develop them in terms of political insight, hoping thereby to serve the Christian community with directives for our political task in the world.

3. We must of course continue to organize in smaller groups around the country, reading, discussing, praying together in order to strengthen bonds among Christians as they seek to understand their political commitments.

4. We must also become thoroughly acquainted with the legislative, executive, and judicial processes. How do things get done politically in our world? Present systems need not be normative guides for the future, but we've got to know what is going on in the sphere of politics in order to ask what the reformation of politics requires. Practicing politicians must be consulted. We should talk with them about their struggles and difficulties, or lack of them, with the existing situation.

5. Groups of politically minded Christians should develop further contact with other similarly interested Christians. Enough organized cohesion needs to exist among groups so that, for instance, when hearings are held in an area, Christians can respond by submitting briefs, and then assist Christians in other localities to do the same.

6. We must be serious about maintaining a biblical vision and identity. We should not become confessionally non-descript and colorless. Development of a clear alternative demands that we take a clear stand and represent a distinct position.

7. We must resist the temptation to become a single-issue movement which tends to gravitate toward vested interests. Rather, guided by what biblical obedience means in the whole political arena, we must look toward a long-range program that works from principles to policies to specific actions, remaining sensitive to whatever new issues may arise.

8. Nevertheless, in organizing our efforts we probably ought to emphasize what Bob Goudzwaard calls "crystallization points." We must identify certain crucial

issues upon which we can focus the attention of the Christian community and use those issues, not as ends in themselves, but as means by which to develop a solid program.

9. We must recognize that this course of action will take us farther than some people are willing to go. Taking organized Christian politics seriously will take us all the way to the inner sanctum of Washington, D.C. If we are really serious about an Association for Public Justice, then we must recognize that much in our present political system is unjust and must be challenged. Not all our efforts will be welcomed by other Christians.

But act we must. The Lord's call to us requires more than words, more than assent, more than confession. It opens the way to bearing fruit, the good fruit of God's new life in Christ: the fruit of peace, justice, reconciliation, and mercy.

Part II
The Context of Service

4

The Bible, Justice, and the State

Bernard Zylstra

At the beginning of his Gospel, Mark tells us that Jesus came into Galilee preaching the good news from God: "The time is fulfilled, and the kingdom of God is at hand; repent, and believe in the gospel!" (Mk. 1:15, *RSV*). The other Gospels report much the same story. The foundation of the gospel is the kingdom of God. At the heart of biblical revelation we discover God creating, judging, and redeeming the world over which he rules.

God's kingdom means at least two things. First, it is the *rule of the Lord* over the entire creation by His Word. The kingdom of God is the Creator's constitutional order for every creature. In the second place, God's kingdom is the *creation itself*. The quality of life in the creation depends on the rapport between the order of the King and the obe-

Bernard Zylstra is Principal of the Institute for Christian Studies in Toronto, Canada, where he also teaches political theory. He is the author of numerous essays on politics and law, and the editor of several books on Christian philosophy, including L. Kalsbeek's *Contours of a Christian Philosophy* (Toronto: Wedge Publishing Foundation, 1975).

dience of His creatures. All creatures are God's servants and are subject to the King's rule.

Of course, much of the Bible tells about human sinfulness—the disobedience of God's human creatures. But that does not deny the reality of God's kingdom. The Bible makes clear again and again that human disobedience is and will be brought to judgment by the King. In fact, the good news of Christ about repentance, salvation, and resurrection could be announced only because Christ suffered God's judgment against sin—the judgment of death.

The resurrection of Christ and the subsequent outpouring of the Holy Spirit on the Church are the final promises that the kingdom of God will be fulfilled in perfect righteousness. Thus, the biblical story of creation, human sin, and redemption in Christ is the story of how God rules His kingdom. And for those who begin to experience life in Christ and who read the Bible there should be no doubt that justice and righteousness are fundamental characteristics of God's kingly rule in Christ. Let us turn, then, to the biblical view of justice.

Justice and the Bible

The first thing to note is that the word "justice" is frequently used in the Scriptures to describe God's relations with His human creatures. Someone has remarked that only a religion whose God is just can make a contribution to social justice, that is, to a "right" relation among people. The Bible tells us unequivocally that Yahweh is a just God. All His ways are justice (Deut. 32:4). How are we to understand this?

The Bible frequently speaks of God's relationship with His people as a covenant. His kingly rule is covenantal. God made many covenants with His people throughout history, and they all came to fulfillment in the final covenant in Jesus Christ. If the covenant is the totality of the relationship between God and His people, between God and His creation, then justice is one of the basic fibers of the covenantal fabric. The covenant consists of two parts: God's command and the human response of obedience or

40

disobedience. If we obey, then our lives will be blessed; we will enjoy a good life. If we disobey, we will be cursed. This relationship between God and His image—His human creatures—is stressed again and again: "Obey my voice, and I will be your God, and you shall be my people; and walk in all the way that I command you, that it may be well with you" (Jer. 7:23, *RSV*).

God's justice consists in His faithfulness to the terms of the covenant. God is just in that He gives His people what He has promised. For this reason I believe that we should not look upon God's grace and God's justice as two relationships which stand in tension with each other. God's grace is not in conflict with, but an expression of, God's justice. As Paul's teachings on justification make clear, God will make sinners *just* again because of Christ's work of reconciliation. This way of looking at the doctrine of justification implies that God will rehabilitate sinners to their original position as loving servants. From the human point of view, we can say that when people accept this justification by faith they can count on it that their life will be made whole again. For God in Christ will now deal with people as restored human creatures who will begin to experience the blessings of the good life that the Spirit gives.

God's justice is revealed in Jesus Christ, whose name already in the Old Testament is: "The Lord is our Righteousness" (Jer. 23:6). This name describes the office of the Messiah who, especially in the prophecies of Isaiah, is pictured as the One who will establish a kingdom of *justice*. "With righteousness He shall judge the poor, and decide with equity for the meek of the earth" (11:4). "He will bring forth justice to the nations" (42:1).

In this framework, we may understand what justice is in human affairs. Justice is one of the ways in which we are to love our neighbors. Justice is an inherent element of the gospel, just as it was in the books of Moses, in the Psalms and Proverbs, and in the prophets. For this reason the restoration of the human community in terms of the covenant between God and humanity implies the restoration of a just society.

It is of course difficult to define precisely what the content of the norm of justice is. Words like equity, fairness, and right hint at the meaning of justice. Descriptions such as that of Emil Brunner may be helpful:

> The Christian conception of justice is . . . determined by the conception of God's order of creation. What corresponds to the Creator's ordinance is just—to that ordinance which bestows on every creature, with its being, the law of its being and its relationships to other creatures. The "primal order" to which every one refers in using the words "just" or "unjust," the "due" which is rendered to each man, is the order of creation, which is the will of the Creator made manifest.[1]

Developing this idea, we may say that the norm of justice requires a social order in which people can express themselves as God's imagers. Said differently, the norm of justice requires social space for human personality. By personality I mean the human self whose calling lies in love of God and love of neighbor. That calling entails the realization of a multiplicity of tasks in history. Justice therefore also requires societal space for our cultural tasks. Moreover, the realization of our human calling also entails the establishment of social institutions, like marriage, the family, schools, industries, and the like. Hence justice requires societal space for these institutions as long as they contribute to meaningful and harmonious human existence. Finally, the realization of our many human tasks and callings involves the use of "nature" and its resources. In view of this, justice also requires such an allocation of material goods that human life is made possible, protected, and enhanced in accordance with its creaturely character, status, and end. In short, justice requires freedom for human service.

Biblical Pointers:

The Bible was written during a time different from ours. The numerous ways in which the Lord told His people

42

about how a just society is to be established are oriented to a largely agricultural setting. Nevertheless, there is much for us to learn.

1. To begin with, the Bible rejects the modern notion of private property. When the Psalmist sings, "The earth is the Lord's and the fulness thereof," he means what he says (Ps. 24:1). In effect, the Lord owns the earth; we can only inherit it from Him and use it, subject to certain conditions. When the people of Israel entered the land of Canaan, it was divided among the various tribes according to their families (Josh. 13). Quite clearly the intent was to make sure that each tribe and sub-group would receive enough to live on. Moreover, if for some reason land was sold, it had to be returned in the Year of Jubilee to its original possessor so that no class distinctions would develop between haves and have-nots (cf. Lev. 24:8ff). In the buying and selling of land our notion of land speculation for profit was entirely absent. "If you sell to your neighbor or buy from your neighbor, you shall not wrong one another . . . but you shall fear your God . . . The land is mine" (Lev. 25:14-23).

2. The blessings of the Lord to one person were looked upon as avenues of stewardship to those in need. In the light of what we said about justice in general it comes as no surprise that both in the laws of Moses and later in the books of the prophets the deprived persons were given special attention. The Lord, as it were, said to His people: "Make room in your society for all my creatures. They are made in my image; they are not blocks or stones or beasts but persons with their own tasks and responsibilities. Now make very sure that they can indeed express themselves as such, that they have elbow room for the fulfillment of their tasks. Make sure that the high are brought low and that the lowly ones among you are protected, restored to new opportunities, to service in my vineyard." Quite concretely this meant that four groups of needy persons are constantly singled out as the special recipients of justice and stewardship: the widows, aliens, the poor, and the or-

phans. Ruth's opportunity to gather food for herself and Naomi, for instance, did not depend upon the personal philanthropy of Boaz. Social concern was built into the fabric of the covenant community. "When you reap your harvest in your field, and have forgotten a sheaf in the field, you shall not go back to get it; it shall be for the sojourner, the fatherless, and the widow; that the Lord your God may bless you in all the work of your hands" (Deut. 24:19).

Relations between rich and poor are treated similarly. The former were clearly told never to exploit the latter. As a matter of fact, being wealthy only increased one's responsibility for those in need. "If you lend money to any of my people with you who is poor, you shall not be to him as a creditor, and you shall not exact interest from him" (Ex. 22:25). The financial dealings between rich and poor could never be such that the poor person might lose the base of his livelihood. "No man shall take a mill or an upper millstone in pledge; for he would be taking a life in pledge" (Deut. 24:6). How could the miller make a living without his tools?

3. The earth could be used but not exploited. There is the notion abroad today that Christianity is responsible for the ecological crisis. Lynn White, for example, has stated that "Christianity . . . not only established a dualism of man and nature but also insisted that it is God's will that man exploit nature for his proper ends."[2] Whatever role Christians may have played in the development of modern natural science, technology, industrial production, and environmental exploitation, the destructive effect of this development is not a consequence of a biblical view of nature. Precisely because nature is also God's creation, our relationship towards it must be one of stewardly concern, of custodianship. We are God's trustees in creation.[3] We must act justly not only toward our neighbors; we must also do justice to non-human creatures. We must respect their potentials and their limits. In the system of Sabbath Years, for instance, described in Leviticus 25:1-7, every seventh year the land was to be given a rest.

44

Humans indeed are distinguished from nature in the Bible; human creatureliness is structurally different from the creatureliness of matter, plants, and animals. But this distinction does not warrant exploitation. It implies human stewardship over available but finite resources. The energy and ecological crises of our day are not a result of biblical demands but a consequence of the rejection of those demands in the Renaissance and the Enlightenment. In these distinctly post-biblical movements of the modern era the finitude that belongs to reality as creation is replaced with the notion of an infinite human potential facing nature's infinite, and therefore exploitable, resources. This notion is foreign to the Bible. The Lord has indeed given us dominion over the world of His hand. He has instructed us to "till" the garden but at the same time to "keep it," to preserve and protect it (cf. Gen. 1:28; 2:15; Ps. 8:6).

The Bible and the State

The biblical conception of the state develops these principles of justice and stewardship. The state arises in a society when the interrelationships between tribes and clans and cities within a particular territory require a central administration for the dispensation of justice. The people of Israel were surrounded by states and empires in which the basis of political unity generally was more a matter of absolute power than justice. When something like a national state appeared within Israel itself we detect immediately the liberating force of the gospel for politics. For in the light of the gospel the king has but one main task, namely, the furtherance of a just society. "Give the king thy justice, O God, and thy righteousness to the royal son! . . . May he defend the cause of the poor of the people, give deliverance to the needy, and crush the oppressor!" (Ps. 72).

It is in this light that we must interpret Paul's famous passage about "governing authorities" in Romans 13. Authority is social power, that is, power exercised by one group of persons over other persons. The Bible clearly recognizes the need of authority in the social order. It speaks freely of the authority of priests, kings, parents, even masters. But it sheds indispensable light on the nature of authority. Authority is office, that is, a channel for the realization of divine norms in a social relationship. This means that "there is no authority except from God," who has established the norms that hold for human life. Moreover, authority must be exercised for the welfare of those subject to it. Paul sums the matter up very succinctly: the person in authority is "God's servant for your good" (Rom. 13:3ff).

For this reason Paul rejects the political absolutism that took on concrete shape in the Roman Empire of his time, when Nero reigned. Political absolutism, ancient or modern, proceeds from the notion that the citizen exists for the good of the state. Paul argues the exact opposite: the state and its authorities exist for the good of the citizenry. This, in a nutshell, is the evangelical, the gospel message for politics, both then and in our own time of unprecedented corruption in democratic regimes. Politicians are office-bearers. They are to execute their executive, legislative, judicial, or administrative offices only for the good of the citizenry. That good is public justice.

Moreover, it should be noted that Paul does not arrive at this conclusion on the basis of conceptions that underlie modern democracies: the notions of popular sovereignty, government by the consent of the governed, government of and by and for the people. These conceptions also make the government the servant of the people. But while government may be "for the people," it is not strictly speaking "of the people." The notion of popular sovereignty in essence develops into the tyranny of the majority, or the tyranny of an elite that can effectively manipulate the electorate at the ballot box. Paul's position points to the possibility of an open political system. But he can do this because he rejects the two major options in western political theory and practice: political absolutism and popular sovereignty. Paul can point to an open political system because he can point to the norm of justice which the government is called upon to realize in all its

46

undertakings.

In sum, we have said that creatureliness is service. Further, that human creatures are to be servants-of-love, both to God and neighbor. Thirdly, that all specific divine norms—like justice and stewardship—are to be looked upon as expressions of love. We now see, fourthly, that the expressions of specific norms may well require certain organizations, like the state. Such organizations, fifthly, require a measure of power to achieve their tasks and offices.

What we should now clearly understand is that the use of power in society belongs to the realm of creatureliness, that is, the realm of service. In the light of the Gospel we can safely conclude that no human organization may escape that realm. If it does, it places itself on a divine pedestal, claiming the kind of power and authority that belongs only to Jesus Christ (Matt. 28:18). The fact that the power and authority of the state is subject to the power and authority of Jesus Christ means that the state must establish a social order where love between human beings is given a political shape. Such a social order is one which can still be described in the traditional terms of public justice. What, briefly, does such an order mean for the kind of world we live in today?

The modern state as we know it is a community of citizens whose government is responsible for the administration of public justice within the state's territory, on the basis of political power, in cooperation with other states for the administration of public justice in inter-state relations. Without discussing the various internal building blocks that go into the makings of a state, we may still ask about the relation between the state and the non-state elements within society. The use of the word "society" is somewhat dangerous, because it can be defined in a variety of ways. A measure of clarity is essential. Some thinkers define society as the sum total of human individuals living within a particular territory, along with the social groups that such individuals have voluntarily formed to pursue certain goals. This is the conception of individualism

47

which holds that the individual person is that basic social entity. The opposite conception is universalism, which holds that society itself is the primary and basic and all-embracing unit, of which everything else is but a part.

Both of these conceptions find the final source of authority and reference *within* society itself. In the biblical setting, the final point of reference and source of authority lies *beyond* society, in the Creator whose will for human beings is revealed in Jesus Christ. Adherence to this biblical vision will entail an alternative conception of society. For when we take a look at a particular society, what do we see? First of all, we notice human beings who do not owe *final* allegiance to any social structure, nor to society as a whole. When we are confronted with a social order which demands a person's entire allegiance, we condemn that social order. Hence we sympathize with the current Soviet dissenters, like the novelist Alexander Solzhenitsyn, who rightly claim that the communist regime does not have the right to control their consciences and the literary expression of their convictions. But in a society we also notice more than human beings. We are confronted with a vast variety of institutions (marriage, family, state), associations (churches, stores, factories, clubs, schools), and inter-personal relations (which occur in market situations, airplanes, museums, street corners, highways, etc.). Quite clearly, individual human beings are not the only social entities. Nor are all of these elements parts of an all-embracing social whole.

In view of this, I provisionally describe society as the horizontal complex of all of these human relationships inter-connecting with each other in a particular culture. The many cross-currents between human beings and social structures in a modern metropolis is a good example of what I mean by society. A metropolis is a mini-society.

The state occupies a place in society, in this horizontal complex of inter-connecting human relationships. The place that the state legitimately occupies in society is to be the *integrator of public justice*. I have to add the word "public" to justice here since there are also instances of *private* justice in society where the state does not—or should not—establish the content of rights. Examples of private legal rights can be found in the relations between private persons, such as the terms of a contract to sell and buy a house. Further, the relations among members within a non-state social structure are to be regulated by private law. Concretely, the relations among members of a family, of a local church congregation, of an industrial work community, of a university, are to be regulated by private communal law. Private communal law is indeed subject to the norm of justice, but it is structurally different from the public legal order which the state is called upon to establish. Private communal law (a) pertains to the members of the specific social structure (a specificity which is non-public), and (b) is dependent upon the "qualifying function" of the respective non-state social structure. For instance, the church order of an ecclesiastical denomination belongs to the category of private communal law: it regulates the relations among members of the denomination and stipulates the ecclesiastically qualified rights and duties and responsibilities of these members. The same is true of industrial law: it regulates the economically qualified relations between members of the industrial work community.

The state, however, is concerned with public justice. It must establish a public legal order. When I use the word "public" with reference to the state, I mean that no person or institution that exists within its territorial boundaries can escape the state's legal order with respect to both the rights and the duties that such a legal order organizes. To put it more positively, the state's divine office is to be the administrator of public justice for *every* person and institution living or domiciled within its territory. The state is the Lord's servant for our good. The content of that good is a regime of public justice.

Public Justice in Society

The norm of justice, as I have said, requires a social space for human creatureliness. A just social order involves the creation of social space for both individual persons and their social communities and associations. It is in connection with "social space" that a Christian conception of rights ought to be developed. For a *right* is that measure of social space that a person or a social structure occupies in society guaranteed by the public legal order of the state.[4]

A Christian conception of human rights finds its foundation in the created character of human life and in Christ's work of redemption. The redemptive work of Christ implies the restoration of human beings to their creaturely status as servants of God. Outside of Christ's redemptive work people have no rights. Because of Christ's redemptive work we are called to fight for the rights of all people, whether they are Christians or not.

When I say that rights are founded in the fact that God *created* human beings, I am in effect emphasizing that people are the image of God. Human rights are not founded in an inherent dignity of human personality, as humanism claims. Human rights are founded in a dignity which comes from the Creator. This dignity, first and foremost, is to be God's imager on earth. This divinely endowed dignity requires a recognition of the unique place and responsibility of human beings in society. In the light of this dignity as God's imager we can say that each person transcends all social structures. No person may be entirely enclosed in or enslaved by any institution.

On this basis we can say that a Christian conception of society is a conception of an *open society*, in which men and women have the right to reach out to God or to what they consider to be their final transcendent "value" to which they desire to render allegiance. Divinely endowed human dignity requires an invincible sphere of freedom for human personality. This "sphere of freedom" is what I call the first range of social space to which each person has a right. The state does not grant rights in this sphere. It acknowledges them. It must protect them. It must enhance them in accordance with the expansion of cultural and social resources in the historical process.

50

A single right is never absolute. Rights must be correlative to duties; the realization of rights is the avenue for the expression of responsibilities. The rights of one person may not violate the rights of others. And the pursuit of one right should not occur at the expense of other rights. There must be a kind of simultaneity in the realization of human rights.

The realization of rights is always influenced by the dominant ideals of a cultural epoch. It cannot be denied that western individualistic liberalism has made a distinct contribution to the realization of rights in modern society: freedom of speech, freedom of association, of contract, etc. However, liberalism looked upon one right as supreme to all others, and that supremacy was found in the "right to property." John Locke, who exercised a great influence especially in the English speaking world, singled out "the preservation of property" as the chief end of government, of civil society (*Second Treatise*, par. 85). The supremacy of the right to property implied the neglect of the realization of other rights; it implied the willing acceptance of a class-society in which the class of property owners was given the protecton of the state while the class of have-nots was left to its own devices. In our time the defense of liberalism and the pursuit of justice are distinctly at odds. This conflict is one of the contributing factors to the disintegration of our society.

The rights of human beings ought to be acknowledged, protected, and enhanced by the state in its dispensation of justice. But rights are not limited to human beings. The institutions which men and women have formed in society—like the church and marriage and the family—and the associations which they have organized—in the industrial sector, the media, and the educational world—also have rights which the state must acknowledge.

The protection of these rights of communities and associations will often require that the state is called upon to prevent the destruction of one "sphere" by another. To put the matter a bit more technically, the state as the integrator of public justice must prevent the violation of the internal sphere of one societal structure by another; it must prevent the development of one sector at the expense of another. We can formulate this a bit more positively: the state must create and maintain conditions that lead to the meaningful and harmonious development of all non-state social structures that contribute to human life in a particular culture. Here, too, the state must prevent friction, oppression, and enslavement.

At this point a biblically sensitive conception of the normative task of the state can make a distinct contribution to the maladjustments that we are confronted with in our society. Implicit in the modern conception is the freedom of industrial enterprise. However, that freedom is never absolute. When the exercise of that freedom endangers other relations in society, the state must intervene, and do so if necessary with drastic measures.

What do we now see in our culture? Its chief characteristic is the prominence of industrial production, made possible by scientific advance, technological invention, and gigantic corporations. The expansion of the production of material goods, and their consumption, is the highest good, the *summum bonum* of twentieth-century civilization in Western Europe and North America. The increase in the gross national product (GNP) has become the chief end of human life, in comparison with which every other cultural purpose is secondary. The religion of production and consumption is the main cause of social disarray. For it permits the corporate industrial sector to encroach upon the legitimate social space of the family, marriage, education, the arts, and the media. As a matter of fact, the very integrity of the state itself is endangered by the nearly uninhibited growth of the economic sector. John Kenneth Galbraith, for instance, has pointed out that the alliance between the world of the large corporations and political institutions makes the proper functioning of the state itself very difficult. The state functions in the first place for the benefit of the corporate sector to the detriment of the rest of society.

The origin of this extremely one-sided cultural development must be found in a specific notion of human progress that gained preeminence since the time of the eighteenth-century Enlightenment. Simply stated, that notion holds that progress consists in the unlimited fulfillment of human material needs. That notion has the character of religious conviction and, since it has become the dominant force in our society, it is not readily dislodged. Especially not if the great majority of politicians of all leading political parties adhere to this conviction.

Nevertheless, I believe that precisely at this point of disarray in our society a revived consciousness of justice and stewardship as presented in the biblical frame of reference can contribute to the alleviation of the ills of which we are all aware but for which a cure is hard to find.

Notes

1. Emil Brunner, *Justice and the Social Order*, trans. Mary Hottinger (New York: Harper & Bros., 1945), p. 89.
2. Lynn White, Jr., "The Historical Roots of Our Ecological Crisis," *Science*, vol. 155 (March 10, 1967), pp. 1203-1207. Reprinted in Francis A. Schaeffer, *Pollution and the Death of Man* (Wheaton, Il., 1970), p. 107.
3. See the special issue of the *International Reformed Bulletin* entitled, *Man: God's Trustee in Creation* (nos. 52-53, 1973), especially the articles by Henri Blocher and Martin Vrieze.
4. In a recent paper I have enlarged this discussion of legal rights. See "Religion, Rights, and the Constitution," presented at the Christian Legal Society's Conference on Law and Religious Freedom at the University of Notre Dame, April 23-26, 1981, and soon to be published in a volume of conference essays.

5

Public Justice and True Tolerance

James Skillen

Politics in our day usually begins and ends with "The People," perhaps in the form of "We the people of the United States . . . ," or "The People's Republic of China," or "the will of the people . . . ," or "return power to the people."

Christian politics begins and ends with "The King of kings and the Lord of lords."

> Great and wonderful are thy deeds, O Lord God the Almighty! Just and true are thy ways, O King of the ages! Who shall not fear and glorify thy name, O Lord? For thou alone art holy. All nations shall come and worship thee, for thy judgments have been revealed (Rev. 15:3-4, *RSV*).

Jesus acknowledged, as we know, that *people* do have political responsibilities and that *people* do indeed belong

James Skillen is the Executive Director of the Association for Public Justice. He is the author of *Christians Organizing for Political Service* (APJ Education Fund, 1980), and *International Politics and the Demand for Global Justice* (Sioux Center, IA: Dordt College Press, 1981).

54

in certain political offices (cf. Matt. 22:15-22; Mk. 12:13-17; Lk. 20:19-26; Jn. 19:11). But in the biblical view of life, human responsibility in earthly politics is never a self-contained and self-sufficient affair of "The People." Human politics is always God's business.

The biblical perspective always places human political responsibility in the context of God's sovereignty and Christ's lordship. The Old Testament revelation placed human politics in the context of the anticipation of One who would come as the Prince of Peace, the Just King, the Righteous Lord, the Perfect Judge, the Mighty God (Is. 9:6-7; 40:9-11; Jer. 23:6; Ps. 82:8; 98:4-9). And when Christ did appear for the first time, He announced boldly that "All things have been delivered to me by my Father" (Matt. 11:27, *RSV*). All authority in heaven and on earth, He said, has been given to Me (Matt. 28:18). Christ has come to establish the rule of His Father over the whole earth (Lk. 4:1-21; I Cor. 15:20-28; Phil. 2:5-11; Col. 1:15-20; Rev. 10:1-16).

The Politics of Grace

The biblical revelation also shows us that the time between Christ's first appearance and His second coming is a time of great patience, long-suffering, and grace on God's part. He is not willing that anyone should perish, and so the call goes out for people to repent and to believe the gospel of His kingdom (Mk. 1:15; II Pet. 3:9). God's gracious patience has considerable significance for politics because Christ does not ask His people to administer any kind of forceful, political separation of non-Christians from Christians. In fact Christ gives the opposite responsibility to Christians. We are to love our enemies (Matt. 5:43-48). We are to look after the welfare of those who might do evil to us (Matt. 5:38-42; Rom. 12:20). We are to pray for God's will to be done on earth as it is done in heaven (Matt. 6:10). In all of this we are to leave the responsibility for separating the wheat from the chaff in the hands of the King Himself (Matt. 26:51-54; Lk. 3:15-17; Rev. 5:1-14).

55

A biblical parable which brings to focus the gracious character of this age is the one in Matthew 13:24-30. Jesus told the parable this way:

> The kingdom of heaven may be compared to a man who sowed good seed in his field; but while men were sleeping, his enemy came and sowed weeds among the wheat, and went away. So when the plants came up and bore grain, then the weeds appeared also. And the servants of the householder came and said to him, "Sir did you not sow good seed in your field? How then has it weeds?" He said to them, "An enemy has done this." The servants said to him, "Then do you want us to go and gather them?" But he said, "No; lest in gathering the weeds you root up the wheat along with them. Let both grow together until the harvest; and at harvest time I will tell the reapers, Gather the weeds first and bind them in bundles to be burned, but gather the wheat into my barn" (*RSV*).

In the entire context of the New Testament, this parable seems to suggest that Christians must not try to establish an earthly state or political community that would be for Christians only or that would be fully open only to those who confess Christian faith. It is not *Christian* justice for Christians to enjoy any political privilege at the expense of non-Christians. Non-Christians must be given every blessing in the political arena that Christians themselves enjoy. Just as the wheat and the tares enjoy the same sun, rain, and cultivation, so Christians and non-Christians should enjoy equally the benefits of God's grace given to the field of this world in the present age.

The Christian view of political justice should be built directly on this understanding of God's gracious patience and love. If this is done, then Christian politics will manifest itself not as the Church's selfish attempt to control the state, nor as an interest-group effort to "get" benefits primarily for Christians, nor as a campaign to flood political offices with Christians so that Christians can control the government for the enforcement of Christian doctrine on the populace.

The biblical view of justice for every earthly creature will mean instead that Christians will work politically for the achievement of governmental policies that will protect, encourage, and open up life for every person and community of people, whatever their religious confession and view of life. Justice in political life cannot be based on the biblical teaching about church discipline since earthly states are not churches. The state is not a community of Christian faith; it is a community of public legal care for all people which must not favor or persecute any particular group or society.

Our difficulty in grasping this biblical perspective is quite understandable considering the history of politics in the West since the time of Christ's first stay among us. The Roman empire did not promote an evenhanded justice which comes from God's grace, but frequently persecuted Christians and Jews. Later when Christianity was accepted by the Roman emperors as the established religion of the empire, these emperors frequently persecuted or discriminated against non-Christians instead of Christians. This was no more just in a biblical sense than the former Roman injustice. The Roman empire in both instances falsely identified itself with *God's* empire, and the emperors wrongly assumed responsibility for getting rid of heretics (rooting up the tares)—a responsibility which Christ gave to no human being.

Still later in history the church gained such strength and prominence that it became the chief power behind most of Europe's politics. "Christian politics" then came to mean "church-controlled politics," and the Roman church leaders assumed some of the same power and held on to some of the same ideas that the Roman emperors once had. Political justice reflecting biblical patience and grace was still not operative for the most part.

So much political debate, warfare, persecution, and turmoil occurred during and after the Reformation when most Christians were still confusing the church's and the

57

state's responsibilities that many people came to believe that political life ought to be organized without reference to religion. Our American political roots go back to this period when people were trying to organize government and politics according to so-called "neutral," non-religious principles. They believed that if they could only keep religion in their private lives and in the churches, away from the political arena where all people participate in common, then religious conflict would not interrupt political life and everyone would enjoy peace and prosperity.

But this was no more "just" than the earlier systems of political organization because not everyone agreed that politics was "neutral" or that religion belonged only to private life. In the political arena, therefore, people were still discriminated against and frequently persecuted if they did not go along with this new idea of a common "religionless" politics.

New Political Religions

What we have seen in the last two centuries is that our supposedly "neutral," "secular" political communities have given birth to the most passionate and unjust *religions* that now control most of these political communities. Nationalism, a religious faith in the nation itself, has become the dominant power in modern political life around the world. Various forms of Marxism, a religion of materialistic humanism, dominate many states, persecuting and discriminating against those who do not confess the party line. Many western democracies, including the United States, allow little or no room for minority participation in politics unless the minorities agree to play by the rules that supposedly keep religion out of politics (and out of the schools) and that keep the majority in charge of directing society. This means unjust discrimination against many people.

In reality what has actually happened is that American democratic nationalism has developed into one of the most powerful "civil religions" in the modern world. It is not

Marxist; it is not Roman Catholic; it is not Protestant; it is not styled after the old Roman empire's elevation of the emperor to the position of God. It is rather a religion of secularized Christianity where the American nation has come to be seen as God's specially chosen kingdom—the political community through which the world will be saved politically. God's will is supposedly revealed through the will of a political majority, and all private religions have their primary place of honor as supporters of the nation's common, unified progress through history as God's nation.

The American civil religion not only leads to political injustice at home, but it promotes injustice abroad in so far as "American interests" dominate world politics and economics. "What is best for America is best for the world," is a slogan in the minds of many American citizens and U.S. officials. On the world scene this attitude operates in much the same way that the dominance of one group operates in the internal life of a nation. It means injustice and discrimination against the poor in favor of the rich, against one class in favor of another class, against one religious group in favor of another religious group.

We can see, then, that politics does not exist as a neutral enterprise. Religion cannot be kept out of the life of states. If a Christian approach of patient, gracious justice does not rule human political life, then some other religious dynamic will control it. If all people are not cared for in an evenhanded way in the public legal domain, then another religious impulse will lead to injustice and discrimination. Christians must wake up to this fact today and recognize that if they are not serving Christ in politics according to the norm of biblical justice, then they are serving some false god that will lead to injustice. In America today we believe that we are doing justice to all people by keeping religion out of politics and letting the majority rule. But actually we are keeping a truly Christian work of justice out of politics only to have a democratistic religion of the people dominate majorities and minorities in a way that oppresses and discriminates against certain people and

59

communities of people. The only answer to the present difficulties facing democratic political systems (as well as non-democratic systems) is to recognize that people are basically religious creatures and that religion can, therefore, in no way be kept out of politics. Political life must be opened up to the full diversity of human religious impulses, and evenhanded justice must be the norm by which this diversity is allowed to live publicly.

A Christian Political Response

In the contemporary world of injustice, both domestic and international, Christian politics will begin with the repentance of Christians who come to see that they have not always been ministers of God's gracious, patient justice to others. Christian politics will grow when Christians begin to take seriously Christ's command for us to love our neighbors. The love command will lead us to be dissatisfied with the unloving injustice of the American civil religion, of Marxism, of church-controlled politics, of nationalism, and of every type of organization of political life which discriminates against some to the advantage of others.

Christian politics will mature in America when Christians recover the biblical vision of the *communal* responsibility they have for others. When we begin to see that the body of Christ is not a "part time" or "private" organism unrelated to the political realities of human life on earth, then we will be able to break away from the *individualistic* conception of political responsibility which dominates our democratic political system. We will then no longer be willing to have the major political parties do all of our politics for us on their own terms—terms which presuppose the individualistic character of political responsibility, the rule of the majority for determining what justice is all about, and the neutral secularity of the political dimension of life. Instead we will be driven by the Spirit of Christ to begin working together as a *political community* and not just as an ecclesiastical community or as an educational community. We will see that politics is our business as a com-

60

munity with a distinct view of life unlike the views that other communities of people have. We will begin to do politics as unto the Lord.

Once we begin, as Christians, to take our political responsibilities seriously, we will be able to take up the complex issues of inflation, poverty, taxation, education, foreign policy, racism, and so forth, in order to examine present government policies and political processes in the light of the Christian norm of patient, gracious, loving justice. Then, as the Lord guides us into a deeper understanding of modern political realities from the standpoint of His merciful justice, we will be able to make the necessary tactical decisions about how we should organize our talents and energies for the service of justice. We may find that the present political system will allow us little room for unique Christian service besides writing and speaking about alternative policies. Or we may find that after considerable labor some significant avenues will open up for our organized efforts to restructure the system and to enact policies and laws of greater justice.

To develop a Christian political option, therefore, we must begin by studying the Word of God together in order to see what it teaches about the kingdom of God in Christ. We must pray and talk together in order to grasp the principles of that kingdom as they hold for earthly politics. We must grow up into Christ so that we can gain a *common Christian political mind*. It is not enough for us to say that we have Christ in common if our lives manifest a confusion of divergent approaches to politics. It is not enough for us to say that we all believe that Christ's kingdom is coming if we live in a way that shows no communal unity in our service of the King. If we are children of the light, then our lives should manifest the communal bond that the light gives to us. Politics is a major part of the life we now live by faith. We need the mind of Christ in us. We need to be renewed in all our thought and life by Christ, including our thinking and living in politics.

Right along with our communal growth as the body of Christ, we must also encourage particular ones among us

61

to give leadership in working out the details of our Christian political option. What are the problems facing modern nations today? What can be done to reform our present systems and policies so that greater justice can be done? What is an equitable tax policy? What is justice in education, or in broadcasting? If we are to get answers to these and thousands of other questions, we will have to have economic, legal, historical, and political experts to guide us. They will need to work full time as part of a Christian team, developing the implications of the biblical view of God's rule in Christ over the whole earth. We must work and pray together for the Lord's guidance in our lives as we seek communally to fulfill our political responsibilities before His face. But to do this we must be sure to recognize the talents and gifts that God has already given to certain ones among us in the area of political understanding. If we do not seek to discover and encourage such men and women to do this special service, and if we do not organize for the support of them, then it will not be enough for us to pray and ask God to help us in our political service. God is already richly blessing us with men and women able to give political leadership. Let us consider how we can be good stewards politically of what God has already given.

Christ is King! Will we now serve Him in our political offices or will we continue to limp between the part-time service of Christ and the part-time service of other gods? Christ calls us to His service with all our heart, soul, strength, and mind.

> And I heard every creature in heaven and on earth and under the earth and in the sea, and all therein, saying, "To him who sits upon the throne and to the Lamb be blessing and honor and glory and might for ever and ever!" (Rev. 5:13, *RSV*).

6

American Civil Religion

Rockne McCarthy

History attests to the fact that in pluralistic societies political authority and power have rarely been used in a just manner. This is particularly true with respect to individuals, groups, and institutions which represent a view of life not shared by those in positions of government responsibility. The unjust use of political authority and power is often directly related to the presence of a civil religion in society. Indeed, the very nature of a civil religion entails the establishment of a nonpluralistic public legal order in society.

In order to demonstrate the existence of a civil religion in the United States, the nonpluralistic structure of the public legal order must be exposed. Moreover, the relationship between an established civil religion and the

Rockne McCarthy is Professor in the Dordt Studies Institute at Dordt College, Sioux Center, Iowa where he teaches history and political science. A popular lecturer and author, he has written (with Gordon Spykman and others) *Society, State, and Schools* (Grand Rapids, MI: Eerdmans, 1981), and with James Skillen and William Harper, *Disestablishment a Second Time: Genuine Pluralism for American Schools* (Washington, D.C.: Christian University Press, forthcoming).

discrimination experienced by individuals, groups, and institutions in American society must be unveiled. Such a task might well appear dubious to many Americans, since most believe that the very strength and uniqueness of their country lies in its pluralism. To assume the pluralistic character of the American public legal order, however, would be a mistake.

Early Development

The separation of church and state is one of the basic assumptions of American thought and society. Many interpret this principle to mean a complete and permanent separation of the spheres of religious activity and civil authority. This interpretation grew out of philosophical and historical developments preceding the founding of American political order.

In the Middle Ages, the Church provided both spiritual and political unity for Europe. During this period the church-state establishment promoted orthodoxy and sought conformity in ways that were oppressive to those suspected of heresy. With the Renaissance and Reformation came the breakdown of religious and political unity in Europe, but, although more churches and states came into existence, individuals scarcely gained in freedom. The various states adopted official religions, and deviation from the creed of the established church often meant persecution.

Among the ideas spawned by the eighteenth-century Enlightenment and the age of republican revolutions was the notion that the only way to achieve social peace was to subdue the passions engendered by sectarian conflict. Many political philosophers argued that this could be accomplished by separating the private life of the spirit from the public life of the state. To do so meant nothing less than redefining the nature of religion by limiting religion to theological and ecclesiastical matters and viewing the rest of life as the domain of nonsectarian activity. The hope was that political stability could be achieved on the basis of a supposedly nonsectarian political order.

Apologists for the political tradition of the Enlightenment have argued that liberal-democratic states have provided social stability along with freedom for individuals and groups to practice their private religious beliefs. One of the claims of this essay, however, is that what occurred in the supposedly nonsectarian political sphere of life was the establishment of a nonpluralistic public legal order based upon an individualist social philosophy. In the vacuum left by the disestablishment of churches, a political ideology *every bit as religious* as earlier established religions gave rise to a nonpluralistic political order. The political thinking of the American founding fathers developed in the context of an Enlightenment tradition which assumed a dualistic view of life and religion.

Historical as well as philosophical considerations were involved in the emergence of an American civil religion. Having long been a haven for various groups of dissenters, the new country faced the problem of extensive religious diversity among its inhabitants. The colonies shared a general cultural heritage from the Old World, but any attempt to establish one particular church at the national level would have subverted the hope for political union. The colonies had been united against England largely on the basis of political and economic issues, and in these areas it was possible in time to arrive at majority opinions. The absence of a denominational majority was an important historical factor which coincided conveniently with the new philosophical assumption that the state represented a rational, nonsectarian agreement among citizens to govern themselves.

We must emphasize again, however, that nonsectarian does not mean nonreligious. As Conrad Cherry remarks, discussing the separation of church and state in America,

the disestablishment of the church hardly meant that the American political sphere was denied a religious dimension. In fact, that dimension so permeates the political, educational and social life of America that it constitutes a civil religion that cannot be identified with Protestantism,

65

Catholicism, or Judaism as such. Americans may be participants in *both* the religious dimension of their civil life *and* one of the traditional Western religions.[1]

While it is true that the federal government did not establish a national church, a nonecclesiastical public faith did come to structure the public legal order of the Republic in a nonpluralistic way. Yet Enlightenment political assumptions, thought by some to be "self evident" nonsectarian truths, are judged by others to be nothing more than sectarian claims concerning human nature and the political order.

Several of the prominent characteristics of the civil religion which developed in America can be discussed under the headings of Civil Theology, Civil Peoplehood, and Civil Institutions.

Civil Theology

At the heart of a civil religion is a civil theology. The Enlightenment produced a liberal (individualist) tradition in which the rights of sovereign individuals are absolutized. This atomistic view of the sovereign individual became the central dogma of the American civil theology and a master assumption of American political thought.[2] Proclaimed to the world at the very birth of the Republic in the Declaration of Independence, the notion of the sovereignty of the individual served as the basic political assumption underlying the Constitution. The Declaration presented the individual as a being who was by nature free, independent, and autonomous. Human beings governed themselves by rationally discovering the "Laws of Nature and Nature's God"[3] and freely contracting together to abide by those laws. The consent of the people thus became the only *legitimate* source of political authority and power. Making the "People" the creators of the state, concludes R.R. Palmer, made possible a revolutionary concept of government in America.[4]

The belief in the sovereignty of the people was set forth in the Preamble to the United States Constitution. The statement that "We the people . . . do ordain and establish" expresses clearly the idea of the people as the *constituent* authority. Through their reason the people discerned the "will of the majority" and formed their government. The process of majoritarian rule, which emerged directly from the doctrine of popular sovereignty, continued in the elected and appointed governing bodies. In America all political authority and power flowed from the people and came to expression through the will of the majority. Alexander Hamilton, for instance, articulates this faith of the people in the people in *The Federalist Papers:* "The fabric of American empire ought to rest on the solid basis of THE CONSENT OF THE PEOPLE. The streams of national power ought to flow immediately from that pure, original fountain of all legitimate authority."[5]

John Locke is recognized as the philosophical founder of the American liberal tradition. In his view of social reality, individuals are sovereign, and, therefore, inherently free of every associational relationship. From such a perspective, all social entities are mere abstractions. Every institution, including the state, is an artificial creation of sovereign individuals and represents the sum total of the individuals who voluntarily compose the institution. Thus, only individuals have rights because only individuals are "real," that is, possess ontological status.[6]

This Lockean view of social reality is not, however, accepted by everyone as a self-evident truth. It represents one of several political perspectives of the social order, all of which are based on certain fundamental religious assumptions about man and society.[7] Nevertheless, an individualist view has so shaped American political thought and judicial reasoning that the public legal order of the Republic has never been pluralistic. For this reason, one may legitimately speak of the establishment of a civil religion in America.

Evidence that an individualist perspective has given rise to a nonpluralistic public legal order in the Republic is not hard to uncover. An investigation, for instance, of the Supreme Court's interpretation of the Constitution regarding such matters as the nature of religion and the rights of associations demonstrates a persistent legal bias on the part of the Court against the recognition of the rights of institutions *as* institutions. Although it is true that associations such as business corporations have been acknowledged to have rights, those rights are recognized either on the basis of the right of *individuals* to associate or on the assumption that institutions are artificial *persons*. Both arguments reflect an individualist and, therefore, a nonpluralistic view because the many institutions that make up a society—business corporations, families, churches, schools, and even the state itself—are not recognized as having civil rights and liberties based upon their *own* structural identity and task in society.

The Court's individualist perspective with respect to the state is evident, for example, in the 1793 case of *Chisholm v. Georgia*. In this historic decision the Justices warned against the danger of state absolutism. But in their argument rejecting state sovereignty the Court assumed that a state was merely an "artificial person" which owed its very existence to the will of individuals. The Court thus let it be known that only individuals are sovereign, and that any other view represented an "unnatural and inverted order of things." The Court continued:

> Sentiments and expressions of this inaccurate kind (implying the sovereignty of the state) prevail in our common, even in our convivial language. Is a toast asked? "The United States" instead of the "People of the United States," is the toast given (sic). This is not politically correct. The toast is meant to present to view the first great object in the union: It presents only the second: It presents only the artificial person, instead of the natural persons, who spoke it into existence.[8]

The Court's view reflects a national acceptance of an Enlightenment liberal view of the public legal order. As Louis Hartz has argued, the Lockean creed became "enshrined in the Constitution" of the United States.[9] This American commitment to the doctrines of individual

68

sovereignty and majoritarian rule impressed Alexis de Tocqueville on his visit to America during the 1830's:

> The people reign in the American political world as the
> Deity does in the universe. They are the cause and the aim
> of all things; everything comes from them, and everything
> is absorbed by them.[10]

At the heart of America's civil religion, therefore, is a
civil theology. The Enlightenment produced an individualist liberal tradition which came to dominate
American thought and to structure the public legal order as
few ideologies anywhere have done. The commitment of
Americans to this tradition made the Declaration of Independence and the Constitution the most sacred
documents of the American civil religion.

Civil Peoplehood

People who share basic convictions about themselves
and the world often manifest their sense of common cause
and identity in what might be called a "civil peoplehood."
For some time scholars have written about Americans'
understanding of themselves as a chosen people, as a
peoplehood.[11] The roots of this belief lie deep in the
American past. The New England Puritans, for example,
appropriating the covenantal language of the Old Testament, believed that they were God's chosen people, the
elect who were creating a new Israel in the New World.
Full participation in the Puritan peoplehood hinged upon
the elect's membership in the covenant of grace, the
church, and the political covenants.[12] Although the
Puritan distinction between the elect and nonelect gradual-
ly disappeared with the secularization of American society,
the concept of a covenanted peoplehood remained a key
element of the national consciousness. By the end of the
eighteenth century the Puritan covenants were replaced by
the founding Republican documents: the Declaration of
Independence and the Constitution. These new inviolable
covenants not only bound the Republic together, but also

identified a new republican peoplehood by establishing the grounds for citizenship.

The very meaning of the term "citizen" was unique in the American context. As R.R. Palmer has pointed out, the modern concept of "citizen" first appeared in the Massachusetts Constitution of 1780.[13] From there it found its way into the Federal Constitution of 1789. John Adams wrote in the Massachusetts preamble: "The body politic is formed by a voluntary association of individuals. It is a social compact, by which the whole people covenants with each citizen and each citizen with the whole people that all shall be governed by certain laws for the common good."[14] Palmer observes:

> The thought here, and the use of the word "covenant," go back to the Mayflower compact. But whence comes the "social" in social compact? And whence comes the word "citizen"? There were no "citizens" under the British Constitution, except in the sense of freemen of the few towns known as cities. In the English language the word "citizen" in its modern sense is an Americanism, dating from the American Revolution.[15]

Adams' terminology, as Palmer remarks, may reflect the influence of Rousseau.[16] The fact that Rousseau's idea of the "citizen" was closely tied to his concept of "civil religion" may provide a clue to understanding the moral-religious meaning of citizenship in the American experience.

In the minds of many Americans and even to some extent in the thinking of the Supreme Court until the adoption of the Fourteenth Amendment, citizenship meant more than being born in the United States or possessing a valid certificate of naturalization. René Williamson suggests that we have "inherited from the Greeks and the French Revolution the feeling that citizenship ought to have something to do with shared ideals and that participation without such sharing is ethically reprehensible and politically unwise." He continues:

We give vent to this feeling when we say of someone: "He is legally an American citizen, but he is not really an American." We feel that an American monarchist would be a caricature of a citizen and that an American Nazi or Communist is not truly a citizen either, the law to the contrary notwithstanding. What we mean when we react in this manner is that citizenship is more than a legal bond and that such people do not and cannot share with us what we consider to be the presuppositions of citizenship. Citizenship means membership in a community, and how can there be community without a common loyalty to shared ideas? This feeling has found its way into our naturalization laws which prescribe not only a willingness to defend the United States but also an understanding of and affection for the Constitution.[17]

If the meaning of "citizen" is ambiguous in the American experience, the meaning of the American Revolution is not. Most Americans at the time interpreted the Revolution as proving conclusively that they and the American Republic (one and the same) were the primary agents of God's meaningful activity in history. Believing themselves to be (pre-)destined by a benevolent diety (whether the biblical God of the Christians or the God of nature of the rationalists) to be freed from England, they also felt called to spread the gospel of republicanism to all people. As early as 1765, John Adams wrote in his diary that, "I always consider the settlement of America with reverence and wonder, as the opening of a grand scene and design in Providence for the illumination of the ignorant, and the emancipation of the slavish part of mankind all over the earth."[18] Such a notion can be found in the sermons of clergymen as well as in the writings of Deists such as Adams and Jefferson.

This messianic vision was implicit in the Declaration of Independence, where, as Albert Weinberg points out, Jefferson was sufficiently confident of his intuition of divine purposes to present the case for American independence as "indubitable dogmas of truth and destiny."[19] Weinberg remarks that "The Americans . . . had faith not only in the justice but also the inevitability of independence . . . . Thus the first doctrine which reflected the nationalistic theology of 'manifest destiny' was that of God's decree of independence.''[20] When the Constitution went to the states for debate and ratification, its defenders were quick to describe its significance in terms of American destiny. As Alexander Hamilton argued:

> It has been frequently remarked that it seems to have been reserved to the people of this country, by their conduct and example, to decide the important question, whether societies of men are really capable or not of establishing good government from reflection and choice, or whether they are forever destined to depend for their political consideration on accident and force. If there be any truth in the remark, the crisis at which we are arrived may with propriety be regarded as the era in which that decision is to be made; and a wrong election of the part we shall act may, in this view, deserve to be considered as *the general misfortune of mankind.*[21]

It is interesting to note that belief in the messianic mission of Americans and America has served as the apologetic for each of the alternating rationales for America's foreign policy.[22] The first of these, expressed as early as Washington's ''Farewell Address,'' is the principle of ''isolationist withdrawal, the conception of innocent nation, wicked world.''[23] America was to be an example to the world as Hamilton had suggested, but only a moral example. To intervene actively in world affairs would be to expose the chosen people and the young Republic to the evil political forces of the Old World from which they had freed themselves. A second doctrine emerged as the American people and the Republic became stronger and more confident. If the lesson of republicanism could not always be taught by the power of moral example, it might be spread by the use of force—especially to peoples in regions adjacent to the United States.[24] This militaristic messianic mission came to full expression during the era of Manifest Destiny. Americans believed that they had a mandate to spread a republican faith and republican institutions to all of North America. It was the destiny (a secularized idea of Providence) of the American people and the Republic to invade and possess new lands and territories. The Mexican war (1846-48), for instance, was seen by many as a means of regenerating the Mexicans by spreading the "good news" of a republican way of life. The same justification had been used many times before to rationalize the taking of Indian lands and possessions.[25]

Born in the revolutionary struggle with England, the American peoplehood matured in the nineteenth and twentieth centuries to include more people. But participation in the peoplehood came at a high price. For many immigrants who came to America during this period, Americanization was more than a legal process. The loss of cultural and group identity was often the cost of being allowed to become members of the peoplehood. But what was the fate of those who resisted Americanization? A consideration of the civil institutions of the Amreican civil religion will prepare us to take up this important question.

Civil Institutions

The American civil religion comprises not only a civil theology and peoplehood, but also key political, social, and economic institutions through which it is embodied, interpreted, and propagated. The limited scope of an essay will permit me to develop this observation only with respect to public schools and political parties.

Public schools have always been one of the key sanctuaries of civil religion in America. The linkage between civil religion and public education is quite evident, for example, in the republican vision of Thomas Jefferson. Jefferson believed in the certainty of moral conscience and human reason, and, like many other eighteenth-century Deists, he rejected the supernatural, choosing instead to interpret Christianity as a rational moral code. He edited the Gospels to produce his own Bible, cutting the genuine sayings of Christ from the spurious, "as easily distinguishable as diamonds in a dunghill."[26] His profound distaste for theology and the church (Anglicanism was the established

73

faith in Virginia) led him to advocate not only the Virginia Bill for Establishing Religious Freedom, but to propose a system of public primary and secondary schools for Virginia and to found the University of Virginia as a supposedly nonsectarian alternative to Virginia's Anglican College of William and Mary.[27]

Nowhere is Jefferson's own sectarian faith more apparent than in his work as the founder of the University of Virginia. In the stipulations for curriculum he chose not to establish a chair of divinity. To do so, he believed, would be to violate the principle of the separation of church and state because the University was endowed by public monies and administered by civil authorities. (The supposedly nonsectarian obligation to develop moral character was placed in the hands of the professors of ethics.) And yet, when it came time to hire the faculty, he wrote to James Madison about the need to find an orthodox advocate of states-rights republicanism to teach law, and declared:

> It is in our seminary that the vestal flame is to be kept alive; from thence it is to spread anew over our own and the sister States. If we are true and vigilant in our trust, within a dozen or twenty years a majority of our own legislature will be from one school, and many disciples will have carried its doctrine home with them to their several states, and will have leavened the whole mass.[28]

As David B. Tyack comments, " 'Seminary,' 'vestal flame,' 'disciple,' 'doctrine,' 'leavened the whole mass'— what are these terms if not the vocabulary of the sectarian."[29]

Jefferson, it should be noted, prescribed the texts to be used at the University of Virginia. The seriousness with which he approached the task is indicative of the fact that a new field of sectarian battle had emerged: theological bigotry was yielding to political intolerance. Jefferson exclaimed:

> There is one branch in which we are the best judges, in which heresies may be taught, of so interesting a character to our own State, and to the United States, as to make it a

duty in us to lay down the principles which are to be taught. It is that of government . . . . It is our duty to guard against the dissemination of such (Federalist) principles among our youth, and the diffusion of that poison, by a previous prescription of the texts to be followed in their discourses.[30]

Jefferson's choice of texts was enough to make a Federalist Virginian such as Chief Justice John Marshall complain that he was being forced by the state to support the propagation of opinions which he disbelieved and abhorred.[31]

Religious heresies did not concern Jefferson; they were in the area of grace, the private sphere of conscience. Political heresies, however, were a different matter, for they involved the area of nature, the public sphere of the American civil religion. Far from being nonsectarian, Jefferson's educational ideas were intimately tied to his hope for redeeming society through republican values.

Jefferson's ideas are worthy of comment because they were shared by those who believed that education was not an extraneous issue but rather one interwoven with a republican faith commitment. Out of this civil "religious" belief the public school was born. During the revolutionary era a common argument arose that republican institutions must rest on "virtue," and thus a growing need was felt for a universal system of public schools to teach the virtues of republicanism. In the first half of the nineteenth century, under the leadership of Daniel Webster, Edward Everett, Horace Mann, and others, the common school movement developed in earnest.

The public school system is presently experiencing a crisis. Older ideals, such as the view of America as an ethnic "melting pot," no longer express a common consensus. Nevertheless, John F. Wilson's remark is historically valid: "the public school system certainly must be viewed as a powerful engine for reinforcement of common religion . . . . School systems are in fact the American religious establishment through their state symbolism, civic ceremonial, inculated values, exemplified virtues, and explicit curricula."[32] Elwyn A. Smith concludes similarly

75

that "the American public school system is the nation's equivalent to the European established church."[33]

Another institutional expression of the American civil religion can be seen in the nature of political parties and the majoritarian electoral system which effectively limits politics to a two-party system in the United States. The emergence of political parties was not anticipated by the founding fathers for at least two reasons. In the first place, political parties were considered evil by almost every writer in the early eighteenth century. This dislike and distrust of parties was based upon the conviction that factionalism was inherently dangerous to political freedom and stable government. Secondly, it was hoped that a common agreement on basic republican principles would make political parties unnecessary. Cecelia M. Kenyon has pointed out that while "Americans have regarded themselves, and have been regarded, as an essentially pragmatic people, . . . the preference for republicanism which crystallized at the time of the Revolution has constituted an ideological, doctrinaire element in their political outlook which has rarely been questioned."[34] The political parties that developed almost immediately in the new Republic, as well as their heirs, have been essentially pragmatic in their outlook precisely because of the existence of an ideological attachment to Lockean assumptions which has united parties in a common political creed. Unlike the ideological debates of European politics, the major debates within American politics have been characterized almost exclusively by functional and pragmatic questions.

Acceptance of Kenyon's thesis need not make one oblivious to the political divisions that have occurred in the course of American political history. It has long been recognized that there have been several turning points in American politics. Most scholars agree, for instance, that the elections of Thomas Jefferson, Andrew Jackson, and Abraham Lincoln represented significant political realignments. And yet it is also evident that in each case the realignment involved positions *within* a Lockean paradigm. The divisions represented differences in the application of republican principles rather than a fundamental questioning of the principles themselves.

Even the election of Lincoln that led to polarization of American society and resulted in civil war represented not a clash between two fundamentally different political ideologies but rather a conflict over which side, North or South, represented the true "faith of the fathers." Hence Jefferson Davis could argue in his inaugural address that, in seceding from the Union, the Confederacy was acting on the American belief "that governments rest on the consent of the governed, and that it is the right of the people to alter or abolish them at will whenever they become destructive of the ends for which they were established."[35] Similarly, speaking with equal conviction at Independence Hall in 1861 on his journey to Washington to be inaugurated President, Lincoln could vow, "I have never had a feeling politically that did not spring from the sentiments embodied in the Declaration of Independence."[36] The American Civil War represented a division within the faithful (the civil peoplehood) over the true meaning of the faith (the civil theology).

While political parties developed as institutional expressions of a civil religion without any public legal mandate, a majoritarian, nonpluralistic electoral system was established by federal and state law. The single-member electoral district emerged out of a liberal ideology, and, like the majoritarian public school establishment, it serves as a powerful instrument to preserve the ideological consensus in American society. This is because the single-member district makes it almost impossible for parties which stand *outside* the ideological consensus to elect someone to office. Since voting for a third or fourth party essentially wastes one's vote, the basic incentive in a single-member district is to vote for one of the major candidates or parties that stand *within* the ideological consensus. Casting a vote for a candidate of a minor party may be symbolically important, but when only the candidate who wins a plurality of votes is elected to office there is little chance to have that vote translated into direct representation.

A direct relationship thus exists between the legal establishment of a majoritarian single-member electoral system and the maintenance of a liberal Lockean consensus in America. The failure of the American system to produce major political parties representing fundamentally different views of public justice, as well as the political and legal restrictions on the implementation of proportional representation, are directly linked to the role political parties and the electoral system play as institutional expressions of a civil religion in American society.[37]

Civil Religion, Civil Rights, and Christian Responsibility

One of the ironies of an Enlightenment ideology is that the concern to protect individual freedom from the authoritarian control of the state has led, in the case of America, to the undermining not only of the structural identity and task of the state but also of many other societal institutions necessary for a meaningful life in modern society. The refusal to recognize the rights of institutions as institutions is a form of discrimination which manifests the ontological assumptions of an individualist political ideology. Such discrimination leads on the policy level to a program of ignoring institutions, of conceding to them no claims of rights *as institutions* in cases involving their very identity.[38]

Moreover, the rights of individuals as well as of groups have not always fared well in the majoritarian, nonpluralistic public legal order ruled by the American civil religion. De Tocqueville was one of the earliest writers to warn against the dangers of a majoritarian liberal tradition. He pointed out, for example, that with respect to religious freedom Americans were in danger of losing their liberty to the authoritarian "voice of the people." Behind the veil of religious toleration, a "tyranny of the Majority" was developing in America. De Tocqueville concluded that faith in public opinion was becoming "a species of religion," and the majority "its ministering prophet."[39]

78

De Tocqueville observed that the majority not only made the laws in the Republic, but also had the ability to enforce majoritarian values. Though *laws* were supported by majority rule, the enforcement of majoritarian *values* was more subtle but no less real.

> The master no longer says, "You shall think as I do or you shall die"; but he says "you are free to think differently from me, and to retain your life, your property and all that you possess; but you are henceforth a stranger among your people. You may retain your civil rights, but they will be useless to you, for you will never be chosen by your fellow-citizens, if you solicit their votes; and they will affect to scorn you, if you ask for their esteem. You will remain among men, but you will be deprived of the rights of mankind. Your fellow creatures will shun you like an impure being; and even those who believe in your innocence will abandon you, lest they should be shunned in their turn. Go in peace! I have given you your life, but it is an existence worse than death."[40]

One who challenged the dogmas of the civil theology was not physically punished but was isolated and ignored by the majority. The person was labeled un-American and "excommunicated."

Given the development of a civil religion in America, one might ask why so few Christians have challenged the dogmas of the civil theology and separated themselves from the false demands of the civil peoplehood and civil institutions. Although the Christian community was heir to the biblical view that Christ is sovereign over *all of life*, many individuals and groups modified this confession by separating life into the realm of grace and the realm of nature, the "spiritual" and the "worldly." This dualism limits the Christian faith to the private aspect of one's life while consciously or unconsciously allowing one's public life to be directed by other norms. This form of religious individualism often took for granted or ignored public life outside the institutional church, and sought rather to build up religious cells of the "saved" within society. By concentrating so heavily on matters of the "soul," a distinctly

Christian understanding of public justice and societal institutions did not develop.

Another factor which made it easy for Christians to accept a majoritarian, nonpluralistic public legal order was that they were the majority. Even if actions and laws were not distinctly Christian, it was obvious that many flowed from the Judeo-Christian ethic. If public schools, for example, were run by the state and inculcated republican values, as Horace Mann and others planned, they also reflected the basically Christian (largely Protestant) feelings of the majority. Roman Catholics and Jews attending these schools frequently felt uncomfortable. The Catholics, especially, began to organize their own schools for which they had to pay the cost while continuing to support public schools through their taxes. Setting up alternative schools was motivated by the Catholic conviction that the public school establishment represented a vehicle for imposing the sectarian beliefs of a Protestant majority upon a minority.

By the twentieth century Americans were becoming more secular in their beliefs. The secularization process was reflected in changing educational philosophies, curricula, textbooks, and personnel in the public schools. Protestant beliefs were being replaced by secular religious ones.

Now many Christians find themselves faced by the hard reality of the American civil religion: the majority rules, and they are no longer the majority. It is of course true that certain aspects of the civil religion are in crisis. The rejection of the melting-pot ideal, for instance, has strained the notion of a civil peoplehood. Civil institutions no longer command the loyalty they did in the past. Nevertheless, despite these developments, fundamental dogmas of the civil religion remain largely unassailed. Basic tenets of the civil theology, such as the sovereignty of the people, are rarely questioned.

Hence the challenge and task facing Christians today is monumental. Christians must demonstrate how a political perspective conscious of its religious assumptions can break the bonds of a civil religion by structuring a truly pluralistic public legal order. Furthermore, Christians must actively work for the civil rights of all individuals, groups, and institutions in American society. The field of education is just one area in which an individualist, liberal ideology has structured a nonpluralistic public legal order which is fundamentally unjust.[41]

The first Amendment to the Constitution prohibits Congress from making any law respecting an establishment of religion. The Supreme Court has ruled in the famous 1963 decision outlawing oral prayer and Bible reading in the public schools that, with respect to religion, "the government is neutral, and while protecting all, it prefers none, and it disparages none . . . . In the relationship between man and religion, the state is firmly committed to a position of neutrality."[42] The Court's assertion that it has discovered a basis for its judicial reasoning which guarantees such neutrality rests on the assumption that the distinction between religious and nonreligious or secular activities can be determined. Yet one may justifiably argue that the Court has come to this conclusion because it has uncritically accepted an individualistic, liberal ideology which assumes, among other things, a secular/religious dichotomy. But such an assumption is self-evident only to those who stand within the liberal tradition. To those who do not, the religious/secular dichotomy is less of a neutral self-evident truth than it is a self-serving sectarian criterion used to secure, for example, public funds for some schools and to deny funds for others.

To the extent that the present system of public education is nonpluralistic it fails to measure up to the standards of a truly democratic institution. More and more citizens and groups are coming to join in this criticism and to conclude that a system of state-supported and administered public education which is fundamentally rejected by individuals and groups, who are, nevertheless, forced by law to support it financially without receiving proportional funding for alternative schools, is a violation of the rights of minorities by the majority. Christians who stand up for their civil rights must do so in the interest of the civil rights of all minorities, whether they be Jews, Black Muslims, Indians, or others whose beliefs necessitate a rejection of the educational context, outlook, purpose, and methods of the currently all-powerful, nonpluralistic, public school system.

What the Supreme Court and other government bodies have failed to realize in cases dealing with religion and the public schools is that the actions of individuals, groups, and institutions are inescapably guided by basic assumptions about human nature and society. Only after this has been realized can genuine neutrality arise which will give proportionally equal and just distribution of tax monies and services to all citizens, groups, and institutions which represent the many different ideological and religious perspectives and peoplehoods existing in our pluralistic society. The state must seek to do justice to the many diverse communities of belief as they concern themselves not only with their special ecclesiastical institutions but with such matters as education, industry, the arts, and the media.

One of the encouraging developments concerning issues of public justice is that individuals and groups from many different backgrounds and perspectives are more carefully questioning the norms of liberal majoritarian democracy. Evidence of this is a renewed interest in the normative character of societal pluralism. For example, *Consociational Democracy: Political Accommodation in Segmented Societies*, edited by Kenneth McRae, is a work that results from political studies of a number of smaller European democracies which reveal that an alternative exists to the commonly accepted classification of western-style democratic regimes.[43]

Discussions in the past have usually contrasted stable two-party systems based on alternating majority governments with more volatile multi-party systems based on fluctuating ministerial coalitions. It is now pointed out by a number of highly respected political scientists that the Netherlands, for example, is characterized by both a stable

82

democratic government and substantial divisions in its social structure, divisions based on broad ideological or religious foundations. In such a "consolidational democracy" (characteristic also of Belgium, Austria, and Switzerland), political parties as well as other voluntary associations such as schools and labor unions are structured so as to acknowledge confessional differences.

This full recognition of the "spiritual families" (Catholic, Calvinist, or the secular religions of liberalism, socialism, or communism) means that no artificial dichotomy is recognized between the religious and nonreligious individual, between religious and secular institutions, or between sacred and profane culture. Full societal pluralism of consociational democracy is to be contrasted with Anglo-American democratic societies which, operating out of a dualistic view of life, encourage pluralism (the freedom of sectarian groups) in the *private* spheres of life (in church, home, etc.) while failing to encourage or fully recognize pluralism in the *public* life of the political community. American pluralism is thus a *limited* pluralism; it does not extend fully into the public legal order.

Clearly, what is needed in order to provide justice for all is a political perspective that gives rise to a public legal order that is more rather than less responsive to the diversified confessional life of modern society. The desire for full public recognition of the legitimate differences among peoples is being voiced at the grass roots of society. Out of the melting-pot myth is emerging a new ethno-religious consciousness from white ethnic groups, such as the Polish, Italians, Portuguese, Hispanics, as well as the Blacks, Chinese, and Indians. Their concern is the same: for equal protection and benefits under the law. Many groups are now demanding full public recognition of their life views in such things as the distribution of federal funds, their own schools, proportional representation in local government and media. Only time will tell if the rise in consciousness of different ethno-religious "peoplehoods" can serve as a foundation for fuller expression of societal pluralism. A political system such as a consociational democracy would, it seems, be more amenable to providing justice for the pluralism of "peoplehoods" in America than is the present liberal majoritarian system.

In summary, I have argued that a civil religion, with a civil theology, peoplehood, and institutions, has dominated American thought and structured an essentially nonpluralistic public legal order for American society.[44] The fact that the present political structure does not measure up to the norms of a truly pluralistic order is indicated by the discontent voiced by individuals, groups, and institutions demanding a fuller recognition of their civil rights. One can expect that the presence and the consequences of a civil religion will become even more apparent in the future. When this occurs there may be an increased willingness to explore how a pluralistic public legal order breaks the bonds of civil religion and allows all citizens, groups, and institutions to fulfill their unique identities and tasks in a free society under law.

Notes

1. Conrad Cherry, *God's New Israel: Religious Interpretations of American Destiny* (Englewood Cliffs, NJ: Prentice-Hall, 1971), p. 10.

2. The eminent historian Louis Hartz discusses the notion of atomistic social freedom as a basic assumption of American political thought in his book, *The Liberal Tradition in America* (New York: Harcourt Brace Jovanovich, 1955), p. 62. In the present essay the terms "liberal" and "individualist" are used interchangeably. As Hartz points out, the very nature of the liberal tradition is that it is individualistic and antistatist. The liberal tradition is to be contrasted to the European conservative tradition which is hierarchically oriented and statist. We have no American conservatives in the European sense, or almost none. In America "right wing" conservatism and "left wing" liberalism are two wings of the same liberal tradition.

3. The phrase in the Declaration of Independence, "The Laws of Nature and Nature's God," testifies to the belief that it was from nature that individuals discovered political truth. In this context, "Nature's God" was merely the necessary hypothesis that Jefferson and eighteenth-century Enlightenment thinkers used to demonstrate that reality was what human reason made it.

4. R.R. Palmer, *The Age of Democratic Revolution: A Political History of Europe and America, 1760-1800*, Vol. 1: *The Challenge* (Princeton: Princeton University Press, 1969), p. 228.

5. Alexander Hamilton, "The Federalist No. 22," in *The Federalist Papers*, introduction by Clinton Rossiter (New York: The New American Library of World Literature, 1961), p. 152. Emphasis in the original.

6. For a more detailed discussion and analysis of an individualist view of society see Rockne McCarthy, "Liberal Democracy and the Rights of Institutions," *Pro Rege* (a faculty publication of Dordt College, Sioux Center, Iowa), Vol. VIII, No. 4, June, 1980.

7. Universalism and Pluralism represent alternative views of social reality. See Rockne McCarthy, "Three Societal Models: A Theoretical and Historical Overview," *Pro Rege*, Vol. IX, No. 4, June, 1981.

8. *Chisholm v. Georgia*, 2 Dallas 419, 1L. Ed. 440 (1793).

9. Hartz, *The Liberal Tradition*, p. 9.

10. Alexis de Tocqueville, *Democracy in America*, ed. Richard D. Heffner (New York: The New American Library, 1956), p. 58.

11. Some of the recent systematic accounts are: Ernest Lee Tuveson, *Redeemer Nation: The Idea of America's Millennial Role* (Chicago: University of Chicago Press, 1968); Russell B. Nye, *This Almost Chosen People* (East Lansing: Michigan State University Press, 1966); and Richard W. Van Alstyne, *Genesis of American Nationalism* (Waltham, MA: Blaisdell Publishing Co., 1970). For many of the relevant documents as well as editorial insights see Conrad Cherry's *God's New Israel*. An older yet penetrating analysis can be found in H. Richard Neibuhr's *The Kingdom of God in America* (New York: Harper and Row, 1937).

12. For a detailed analysis see Perry Miller, *The New England Mind: The Seventeenth Century* (Boston: Beacon Press, 1961), pp. 365-462.

13. Palmer, *The Challenge*, p. 224.

14. *Ibid.*, p. 223.

15. *Ibid.*, pp. 223-224.

16. *Ibid.*, p. 224. Adams was familiar with Rousseau's *Social Contract*, and Book I, Ch. VI may have provided a specific source for Adams' concept of "citizen."

17. René De Visme Williamson, *Independence and Involvement: A Christian Reorientation in Political Science* (Baton Rouge: Louisiana State University Press, 1964), p. 171.

18. Quoted in Tuveson, *Redeemer Nation*, p. 25.

19. Albert Katz Weinberg, *Manifest Destiny: A Study of Nationalist Expansionism in American History* (Gloucester, MA: Peter Smith, 1958), p. 16.

20. *Ibid.*, pp. 16-17.

21. Alexander Hamilton, "The Federalist No. 1," p. 33. Emphasis mine.

22. Tuveson, *Redeemer Nation*, p. 213.

23. *Ibid.*

85

24. *Ibid*.

25. For a radical revisionist interpretation of the Atlantic Coast Indians' encounter with white settlers during the colonial period of United States history, see Francis Jennings, *The Invasion of America: Indians, Colonialism, and the Cant of Conquest* (New York: W.W. Norton & Co., 1976).

26. Quoted in David B. Tyack, ed., *Turning Points in American Educational History* (Waltham, MA: Blaisdell Publishing Co., 1967), p. 90.

27. For a full examination of Jefferson's religious perspective and its role in shaping a vision of public education in America, see Rockne McCarthy, James Skillen, and William Harper, *Disestablishment A Second Time: Genuine Pluralism for American Schools* (Washington, D.C.: The Christian University Press, 1982).

28. Quoted in Tyack, *Turning Points*, p. 91.

29. Tyack, *Turning Points*, p. 91.

30. Quoted in Tyack, *Turning Points*, p. 91.

31. Tyack, *Turning Points*, p. 91.

32. John F. Wilson, "The Status of 'Civil Religion' in America," in Elwyn A. Smith, ed., *The Religion of the Republic* (Philadelphia: Fortress Press, 1971), pp. 7, 8-9. For an analysis of the religious character of public education in America see Rousas J. Rushdoony, *The Messianic Character of American Education* (Nutley, NJ: The Craig Press, 1963). A convenient collection of documents can be found in Rush Welter, ed., *American Writings of Popular Education: The Nineteenth Century* (Indianapolis: The Bobbs Merrill Co., 1971).

33. Elwyn A. Smith, ed., *The Religion of the Republic*, p. viii. The same point was made much earlier by Sidney E. Mead, in "Thomas Jefferson's 'Fair Experiment'—Religious Freedom," p. 68. This is one of a collection of Mead's articles published together under the title, *The Lively Experiment: The Shaping of Christianity in America* (New York: Harper and Row, 1963).

34. Cecelia Kenyon, "Republicanism and Radicalism in the American Revolution: An Old-Fashioned Interpretation," in *The Reinterpretation of the American Revolution, 1763-1789*, ed. Jack P. Green (New York: Harper and Row, 1968), p. 305.

35. Quoted in Ralph Henry Gabriel, *The Course of American Democratic Thought* (2nd edition, New York: The Ronald Press, 1956), pp. 121-122.

36. Abraham Lincoln speech, Philadelphia, February 22, 1861, in *Abraham Lincoln: Selected Speeches, Messages, and Letters* (New York: Holt, Rinehart, and Winston, 1957), pp. 136-137.

37. For a more detailed analysis of the differences between a proportional and majoritarian system of representation as well as the history of proportional representation in the United States, see Clarence Hoag and George Hallett, *Proportional Representation* (New York: The Mac-

Millan Co., 1926); James Skillen, "Justice for Representation: A Proposal for Revitalizing Our System of Political Participation" (Washington, D.C.: Association for Public Justice, 1979).

38. Well-known sociologist Peter Berger and *Worldview* magazine editor Richard Neuhaus argue that freedom is weakened by public policies and court decisions which undercut the position of nonpolitical institutions in society. See *To Empower People: The Role of Mediating Structures in Public Policy* (Washington, D.C.: American Enterprise Institute for Public Policy Research, 1977). See also Rockne McCarthy, "Liberal Democracy and the Rights of Institutions."

40. De Tocqueville, *Democracy in America*, p. 149.

41. *Ibid.*, p. 188. De Tocqueville's reference is to an author, but it is clear that the example holds for anyone who challenges the will of the majority.

41. For a detailed look at the forces behind the rise of the American school system and a critical assessment of that system together with proposals for change, see Rockne McCarthy, *et al.*, *Society, State, and Schools: A Case for Structural and Confessional Pluralism* (Grand Rapids: Eerdmans, 1981).

42. *School District of Abington TP., PA. v. Schempp*, 374 U.S. 203 (1963).

43. Kenneth D. McRae, ed., *Consociational Democracy: Political Accommodation in Segmented Societies* (Toronto: McClelland and Stewart, 1974). See also McRae's Presidential Address to the Canadian Political Science Association in 1979, "The Plural Society and the Western Political Tradition," *Canadian Journal of Political Science*, Vol. XII, No. 4 (December, 1979), pp. 675-688.

44. For different interpretations of the meaning of civil religion in America see Donald R. Cutler, ed., *The Religious Situation: 1968* (Boston: Beacon Press, 1968), and Russell E. Richey and Donald G. Jones, eds., *American Civil Religion* (New York: Harper and Row, 1974).

7

Christian Action and the Coming of God's Kingdom

James Skillen

How should our political action be guided by our faith in the coming of God's kingdom? How does our knowledge of the future impinge upon our political life in the present age? To answer these questions, we must first understand that the biblical revelation calls us to respond to God with our whole life in the service of our neighbors. It does not allow for either "quietism" or "activism." By "quietism" I mean an attitude that has, unfortunately, characterized Christians for centuries, namely, a sense of hopelessness about life in this world. Or, if not hopelessness, at least a strong doubt that Christians can have much effect on life in this world, especially on political life. The consequence of such an attitude is for Christians to hold back, quietly, from serious reforming engagement in the affairs of this world. By "activism" I mean almost the opposite attitude—a conviction that Christians can change the world to such an extent that the primary motivation for their efforts here and now is the hope of transforming this world into the kingdom of God through political, economic, educational, and evangelistic good deeds.

By contrast, the biblical picture of God's people living and working expectantly for the coming of the kingdom is neither quietistic nor activistic. It is a picture of God's people working diligently in all areas of life, including politics, knowing that God will bring all things to completion and fulfillment in His kingdom through His Son, Jesus Christ. Our attitude ought to be one of confidence that in Christ there is an intimate connection between this world and the coming kingdom, that there is no radical discontinuity between our labor in this world and our fulfillment in the next. But the coming kingdom is in God's hands not ours.

The Creation's Sabbath Structure

This is directly relevant for politics, because it is in political life that quietism and activism show up most clearly among Christians. In an attempt to overcome this problem, I would like to consider a particular characteristic of the biblical revelation that begins to unfold in the very first chapter of Genesis. That characteristic is the seven-day, sabbatical structure of the creation. Although the first chapter of Genesis in the English Bible concludes with the end of the sixth day, the whole story of creation in the Hebrew text includes the description, in 2:1-4, of the seventh day, the sabbath rest into which God Himself entered after His labor. This sabbatical pattern as a whole forms the context for God's revelation of Himself to Israel and for the final revelation of Jesus Christ.

In the Genesis passage we see that the days of creation are quite distinct in character. There are days and nights, and the day of the sun and the moon is a different day from the day of the plants; the day of plants is different from the day of separation between waters and dry land. Moreover, we see that the day of man, the day of human beings, is a different kind of day than the sabbath rest of God—the day in which God enters into His rest. Yet at the same time, it is also clear that all of the days are integrally wrapped up together as parts of *one* creation. The creation is not a separate six-day entity, contained in itself and set apart from God's seventh day of rest. God's resting is directly related to His laboring. The seventh day is not another world; it is the climax, the completion, the culmination of God's one creation.

Or, one could say from another angle that human creatures are quite "other" than the creatures made on the other days. We are not plants or fish or stars. Nevertheless, the day of human life is wrapped up with all the days of the creation. We cannot live without the plants; we cannot live without the dry land and the water. And we cannot live without anticipating the day of climactic fulfillment and rest. There are obvious differences among God's creatures. Water is not sunshine; humans are different from plants. But they are all part of a single unified, interdependent creation that exists to reveal God and to enjoy His sabbatical blessing.

As the biblical story unfolds, this picture provides the setting for our human place and task on earth. In the beginning God gave His image, male and female, the responsibility of dominion and stewardship in the creation. We have our identity and purpose in the context of caring for the rest of the creation, caring for one another, and looking forward to the culmination of all things in God's final day of rest. Abraham looked ahead to the city that God Himself would make (Heb. 11:10). The author of the letter to the Hebrews, particularly in chapters 3 and 4, develops this dynamic image. A sabbath rest, he says, has been promised to the people of God; it is the very thing that they have been anticipating from the beginning. And the rest which has been promised them is God's own sabbath day (Heb. 4:1-11).

We need to keep this revelation in mind in order to understand politics and the future. The coming age is a new age, but it is the completion, the fulfillment of this age. It is the restoration of what was lost in our sin, but also the completion of the creation which has existed from the beginning as a seven-day creation. In Christ we have been given the promise of entering God's rest. Therefore, the final triumph, the final coming of Christ, the new heaven and new earth, the new age—all of those aspects of

90

the future which might seem to suggest a discontinuity, a break with the present world, are really aspects of sabbatical fulfillment of God's single creation. The radical newness of the future is not a symbol of the destruction of God's first creation but rather the sign of perfect fulfillment of what God has been doing from the beginning. A close continuity exists between what we are doing now and what we will be doing then in politics as in the rest of life.

Let me give just one simple illustration. Some Christians have emphasized the discontinuity between this age and the next age so strongly that they expect heaven to be the end or the negation of marriage. After all, they say, doesn't the Scripture say that in heaven there will be no marriage or giving in marriage (Matt. 22:30)? But for Christians who are enjoying loving marriages now, such a heaven might not be a very exciting prospect. Heaven, in that sense, represents the end of marriage. It is a negation of life in this world. It seems to me that this outlook is fundamentally unbiblical. Granted, heaven, as the new age, will be unlike what we now know in the sense of being the perfect completion and fulfillment of life in Christ. However, everything in the Bible testifies that the new age is going to be the perfect fulfillment of all that God has intended for His creation and for His people. Marriage, then, will be *more complete* than it is now. Marriage will not be negated but fulfilled.

Of course, the biblical revelation does testify to the purging fire of judgment. There is judgment and trial by fire, and only gold will get through to the kingdom. We can be thankful that all the chaff, all the rottenness of our sin, will be destroyed. A judgment is coming which will indeed create a radical discontinuity in our lives because the sinful nature is going to be put away once and for all. But the creation of God's design, the meaning and purpose of the seven-day creation, will unfold to its completion in God's sabbath day. The new age is not the end of this age but merely the end of sin and the end of an unfulfilled creation.

Sojourners and Homesteaders

With this general sabbatical framework in mind, we can look briefly at two important images or metaphors that are frequently used to describe the life of God's people in this world: the metaphors of "sojourners" or "pilgrims" and "householders" or "homesteaders." These metaphors are in fact related, I will suggest, because the Scriptures encourage us to think of our sojourning not as sojourners but as homesteaders, and to think of our homesteading not as homesteaders but as sojourners. Let me explain.

If we have the quietistic idea that this is *not* our Father's world or that we do not really belong here, then the sojourning attitude will be one of looking forward to getting out of this world. We will walk through the world with no intention of participating too seriously in its political life, for example, except in so far as it is necessary to do some minimum amount of work to survive or to look after ourselves. We will walk through the world leaving all kinds of good creaturely things behind, including the full creaturely meaning of political life. We will always be looking forward to another world to live in because this one does not seem very much like home.

It seems to me, however, that the idea of sojourning ought to be one of always moving on toward the fulfillment of what we now have, of what we now are in God's creation. This idea is connected in the Scriptures with sojourning in the midst of sin or in the midst of persecution; it is sojourning in the midst of deformity. But sojourning is for those who know that they ought to break with sin and occupy the land, who sojourn as homesteaders who belong *here* and not elsewhere. It means to take politics seriously as an important dimension of our lives that must be developed, realizing that the final fulfillment of God's perfect kingdom of justice will gather into it all the glories of the earthly kingdoms and all the goodness of our labors for justice in this age. God did not intend that Israel should walk forever in the wilderness. Israel sojourned in the wilderness so that God could teach His people how to leave sin behind and to become responsible homesteaders. They were in the wilderness *not* so that they could adopt a permanent attitude of having no home, but so that they could learn what it would mean to live properly in the city of God when they finally got into the place where they would build their homes.

On the other hand, our homesteading in this world ought to be as sojourners. This age, even in its creaturely goodness, was not designed to remain forever. The sixth day is not the last day; God's sabbath rest is our final destination. If we think of ourselves simply as homesteaders, that is, as those who were put here on earth to remain permanently as caretakers, then we lose sight of our present disposability and our ultimate destiny. That is wrong. From the beginning we were meant to be the kind of stewards and homesteaders who are always anticipating and moving toward the final sabbath. From the beginning there has been an eschatological direction to the creation. From the beginning God has been calling us toward the fulfillment of the works of our hands. In this regard our homesteading in this world is a homesteading that looks ahead for more. We are homesteading as Abraham's sons and daughters, looking ahead to the heavenly city that God is building for us and through us in Christ Jesus. We are homesteading as sojourners.

We have to be both sojourners and homesteaders, but we have to be both at the same time. We must not be divided, thinking of ourselves at one time simply as sojourners in a world that is not really ours and at another time as homesteaders in a world that has no future to it. We are always on the move, looking forward to the creation's fulfillment, but we do so as people who are gathering up all the creation with us as we go; we are leaving nothing behind but are carrying everything with us into the kingdom. We were meant for this world and it was meant for us. There is only one creation. And yet all of God's good creation is intended for a final sabbatical fulfillment.

It is important for us to return regularly to the biblical context of these metaphors because it seems to me that a primary assumption among Christians, historically, has been that this world and the next are more discontinuous than continuous. We have acted as if political life is somehow separated from or set over against, the coming kingdom of God. For example, the early church was influenced significantly by a movement called "gnosticism." The gnostics were convinced that this world is fundamentally a death-trap. We are locked into it at the moment but we do not belong here. A special knowledge (gnosis), however, has been given by revelation which shows some people how to escape from this world. The world of matter, the physical, visible world that we see and feel is an evil thing, a prison. The true world, the ultimate world of freedom and light, is the spiritual world—a higher realm. But there is no way of escape out of the visible world into the spiritual world without the special knowledge which is passed on in a secret fashion.

Gnosticism influenced Christianity to the point where some Christians began to think of Christ as the revealer of the special knowledge that shows how to escape from this world, the One who brings the special "gnosis" for the few and gives them the secret of escape into the realm of spiritual light. That influence led to a long tradition of quietism in Christian circles. This world is a rotten place, at least politically speaking. Politics is part of the evil world in which we now live. From this viewpoint Christ offers human beings a way out of this world into a heavenly kingdom. Christians are spiritual sojourners in a bodily, material prison.

Modern Ideologies

The same attidude in modern secular forms has had an important influence on what might be called the secularistic gnostic movements of our day, including Marxism. At first glance, Marxism of course seems to have nothing in common with Christian quietism. But in a Marxist vision of the world, the world is also fundamentally corrupt; it is fundamentally malstructured and disorganized. Capitalism is the highest stage of the social distortion and disorganization of human life in this world.

Human beings have to escape from it. But what is the special knowledge, the special light that can show the way out of the trap? A special revelation no longer comes from on high, and certainly no Messiah, other than Marx himself, comes to show us the way to escape. Rather, for the Marxist, the special knowledge is a refined science that allows us to know with final certainty the inner purpose and outcome of history. And by means of this special scientific knowledge we can look ahead to the final change of this world. But since Marx anticipated no escape from this world, his gnostic ideology turned into a secular activism, that is, a program for radically remaking the present world, including human nature. From the Marxist viewpoint, we live in an almost inhuman trap, a trap of social and economic darkness; but after the revolution we will have a world of perfect harmony and peace in which everyone will give according to his ability and take according to his need. It is a picture of an earthly paradise—a picture of heaven brought down to earth by human revolutionary means. It is not a heaven into which we escape because of the work of a gnostic Christ but a heaven that we ourselves make through the revolution. Thus, out of the influence of ancient gnosticism there arose first a "Christian" quietism about this world and then a secularized activism represented by such movements as modern Marxism.

But another reversal has also taken place in modern history. In the twentieth century we can see the transition from "Christian" quietism to a "Christian" activism. The social gospel movement, broadly speaking, was driven by a vision of the kingdom of God coming in this world. It would come, however, not by way of a climactic reappearing of Christ, but through the growth of democracy and economic equality in the world, achieved through human efforts. Once democracy had made its full progress through the world, once equality had been achieved in all respects, then the kingdom of God would exist. The social gospel gave a new impetus to people from a Christian tradition to work for the advancement of democracy and equality. As a consequence, "Christian" activism spread throughout much of Christendom—an activism that is not much different in appearance from secularistic activism.

In recent decades, moreover, yet another reversal has been taking place. I would call it the transition from secular activism to secular quietism. This attitude shows up in the writings of Robert Heilbroner, Jacques Ellul, and others, and it comes to expression in the pessimism of the average man and woman in the street. The deterministic forces of nature and technology, in this view, control the development of capitalism and socialism, the nuclear arms race, ecological destruction, and the computerized society so completely that human beings can no longer halt the developments set in motion centuries earlier by their predecessors. We are heading toward a dead end and there is no turning back. This world is a hopeless mess. There is no escape. Such an attitude leads, in practice, to political apathy and quietism—not a quietism that hopes for a new and better world created by God for those who escape from this one, but just a quietistic pessimism about the present earthly existence which is all there is. Reforming efforts by human beings are useless. Political action, even revolution, cannot change the world or the direction in which it is heading. We are locked into this world and there is nothing we can do about it, so we might as well sit back and hope for the best.

All these forms of quietism and activism are in some sense deformities. They do not express a biblical attitude of expectancy. They are expressions of hopelessness, political hopelessness, because they must give up hope either about this world or the next. The Christian quietists —those who are Christians but influenced by a quietistic attitude toward this world—have hope for an escape from this world. They live by the hope that Christ is coming, that He will relieve them of this rotten world, and that He will lift His people out of it. But to have that hope they must give up hope about this world. The hope for escape goes hand in hand with the belief that earthly politics is a lost cause.

The secular activists, on the other hand, still have faith that the world can be transformed, but their hope for transforming this world goes hand in hand with relinquishing all hope about another world. For the Marxist, it is absolutely essential to give up "religion." The chief thing that holds human beings back from radically changing this world is their belief in another world. If people still hope that somehow God will come to relieve them of their earthly problems, then there is no possibility of getting them organized to change this world. As long as they hope for some outside intervention, as long as they believe that God will give them a better life in some other world, then, says the Marxist, it is not possible to be hopeful about the radical change of this world. It is necessary to give up hope for another world in order to become hopeful about this world.

Politics of Hope

If various forms of quietism and activism have such a strong influence on both Christian and non-Christian thought today, what can we do? Is there a biblical hope for politics? Is there a politics of hope that is biblical? Is there a politics of expectancy that grows out of the biblical vision of God's coming kingdom? I am confident that such a hope exists and is justifiable. It is dependent on the sabbatical structure of the creation in which Christ is revealed to us, not as one who provides an escape route from an evil world, but as the Lord of history. Politics is not a dirty part of this world that God has been unable to reconcile with His purposes for creation. At the same time, politics is not something that we have been given to do as human beings in order to try to create a final utopia in this age. Political power is not a tool by which we are supposed to redesign the world. Instead, political life is part of our human stewardship, under the sovereign Lord of history. Political life as an expression of our humanness is just as important for us as family life, educational life, and agricultural life. None of these aspects of earthly life are permanent in the sense that they will exist in the same way forever and ever. But they all express what we are as God's image in community: they are dimensions of our sabbath-oriented earthly life.

The biblical revelation assures us that history *will* be fulfilled. This means, among other things, that justice will be accomplished. The prophets announced Christ's coming as the arrival of a righteous and just King. Christ is King! Kingship is a political designation, a political office. He comes as the One who is going to bring justice. The fact that the kingdom was at hand in His first appearance meant that the coming of His justice was at hand as well. As Christians, we can count on the fact that justice will finally be established. The One who makes things right and just has come; He has already begun the harvest of justice. His resurrection, which is the firstfruits of the *one* resurrection, is the firstfruits of the fulfillment of justice. The One who was raised was not just a slaughtered lamb; He was the King. Since the King has come among us, we are those who look forward to the completion of His kingdom of justice.

If the kingdom of justice is *Christ's* kingdom, then it is clearly not a kingdom that *we* design and construct. Our labors for justice will be gathered into it, incorporated into its final shape, but it is Christ who does the gathering and incorporating. He is King of the Kings of this world and is going to inaugurate the kingdom to complete all kingdoms. Christ is not the King of some other world. He is the King and Judge of this world. He told His disciples that "All authority has been given to me in heaven and on earth" (Matt. 28:18). At that point He was saying, "This is my Father's footstool" (see Isaiah 66:1); He had put His feet on it. He had dwelt among us, and He was laying final claim to the earth. His final revelation of justice will bring this world to its fulfillment.

Hence we need not have a divided understanding of our life in this world—on the one hand as Christians with a hope of Christ's coming, and on the other, as citizens with earthly political responsibility. Instead, we should have an integral sense of *one* life in *one* world under *one* King. The

Christian gospel is not a gnostic escape mechanism. We cannot escape politics, nor should we try to do so. Politics is part of what we are. But at the same time, even in politics, we are not locked up into a closed world of purely human deeds. Politics is not a world solely of human action. All that human beings do, even in deformity, is subject to the judgment and redemption of the King. He never lets us get away from Him. Therefore Christians can live in this world completely, without reservation, without holding anything back, without longing for a means of escape. But we can live in this world with quite a different attitude and approach than those who think that politics is merely a human affair. It is not merely human. This is God's Kingdom; this is God's world. Kings do not rule by human appointment alone; Presidents do not obtain their offices simply because they win electoral races. They hold their offices under the providential judgment of the King. We can count on that. We can do our politics, and think politically, and act politically in that light, in obedience to the King, because we know that this is His kingdom.

Thus, we do not have to give up on politics; we can be hopeful and expectant because the King has come and true justice will be established. At the same time we must really *do* politics. One ought not to say, "I'm expectant, I'm expecting the King to come," and yet not be busy with part of the King's business. A pregnant woman cannot be expecting a baby without being busy with the preparations for her baby's arrival. If we truly expect the second coming of the Lord and the fulfillment of His kingdom, then everything in creation will be caught up in our preparation for the coming of the kingdom. We cannot say, "We have to be busy with evangelism, with Christian education, and with our church work because the King is coming," but at the same time say, "We can leave politics alone since the King does not care much about rotten earthly politics." That would be to act like a cook who doesn't care about a dirty kitchen or a librarian who doesn't care about the order of the books. No, the King is coming to bring His whole creation to fulfillment and to restore it to perfect

99

righteousness. Therefore we must be busy as citizens with all that pertains to political life so that justice might shine through in our preparations.

Politics of the Kingdom

Now to summarize and organize the argument above, I would say that stewardly expectancy or expectant stewardship in politics should mean at least five things if we are paying attention to God's revelation.

First, we can expect with confidence the full harvest of justice in God's kingdom. The firstfruits of justice are in, and the harvest will soon be completed. The Lord has spoken, and His word is trustworthy. The full harvest, including the establishment of perfect justice throughout the earth, will be achieved. Anyone who does not live with that hope and expectancy has not understood the gospel. Any political action based on some other hope or on hopelessness is not Christian political action.

Second, we can do our politics as part of a true attitude of expectancy by asking what our responsibilities for justice are here and now. We need not speculate about the future or about the schedule of the end times. Our political responsibilities have nothing to do with being able to interpret all the details of the Book of Revelation correctly. Nor is the question for us: "How much of the world can we change radically in the near future?" or "What kind of human utopia do we want?" Those are the wrong questions. The correct question is "What is our responsibility for justice in the situation that is before us?" Every nation and society exists in a particular historical context with certain powers and capabilities, certain problems and prospects, certain deformities and justices, both domestically and internationally. Most of us who are American citizens enjoy relatively great freedom and opportunity. What will we do with all of that? What should we be doing to see that greater justice for all is done now? We can ask these questions and exercise real responsibility because we know who the King is and what He is doing. We do not have to ask, "Can we do it?" The King is coming; justice will be established; that is all we need to know in order to get busy.

In the third place, we have the opportunity as expectant ones to point to the dead ends of political life in our present world. To do so will not be likely to guarantee our political popularity. Most politicians avoid this task like the plague. They cannot afford to let people think that there are any fundamental problems that cannot be solved by those in power. But Christians should not hesitate to expose the patterns of injustice that people and nations have established. Look closely at the way Americans are conducting themselves politically these days. Look critically at the public policies being implemented. Almost everyone knows that something is wrong. Look at the mess we are in environmentally, economically, and in the supply of energy, to mention only three. Surely we must not persist in the present course without delivering a word of warning and true hope. Precisely because we may know what true justice is, we can be fearless in exposing the dead ends of contemporary politics.

We can come with a critical word, moreover, because we can offer more than mere criticism. We are not prophets of doom, but prophets of life. The reason we can be realistic is because we believe in repentance from sin. We believe in a real judgment that will condemn injustice, and therefore we are remiss if we do not warn of the coming judgment. But we believe in the restoration of real righteousness, in true healing of broken lives, and in the setting right of every broken human relationship. That is the nature of our King and His kingdom. He is Judge *and* Redeemer. And, as we have said before, His kingdom is not just for another world but for this world. He will show us how to live justly here and now. We know that the truth about justice and peace is not a gnostic secret but a public revelation that God wants to give away freely to those who will acknowledge His kingship. It is not necessary for people to endure injustice if they will repent and heed the King.

In the fourth place, we can work concretely in the political arena for real change now. Our task is not simply

101

to get clear in our minds what our responsibility *ought* to be. We can expect that obedience to God's norms will have consequences in our immediate political life. We do not need to have any assurance beforehand that our efforts will dazzle the world or turn out perfectly. Our job is not to *bring* in the kingdom but to respond as good stewards who by God's grace are *already in* the kingdom. The aim of our political responsibility is not to reorganize the world once and for all, but to minister to all our neighbors in a political way, demonstrating that God's justice brings peace, well-being, happiness, and fulfillment. In the light of God's norms of justice and stewardship, in the light of the coming of His kingdom, we are confident that by looking at the dead ends in our society and by beginning to suggest changes that will lead to greater justice, we can go to work concretely and usefully here and now.

Since we are homesteading sojourners in this world, and since many of those who have political power do not acknowledge the true King, we might only lose our heads in real political action. But that is no problem. Such results would only strengthen the whole body of Christ worldwide. The blood of martyrs has never been a hindrance to the coming of the kingdom. We should have no fear. On the other hand, we must not be surprised or disappointed if God arranges positions of great influence for some of us as He did for Joseph and Daniel. With or without great political power, our aim must be to do justice in this age as part of our expectant labor for the coming of the kingdom. It does not matter whether we lose our heads or not. We are the only ones on earth free enough to be able to rejoice if we lose them and to rejoice if we keep them. But our real rejoicing can come forth from the fruits of justice. We must weep if justice is not done. Thus it is worse for us to hold political power and not do justice than for us to lose our heads trying to do justice.

Fifth and last, we can work with true expectancy in politics as those who know that our works will follow us. This is something not emphasized enough in our circles.

102

Moses prays in Psalm 90: "Lord, establish the work of our hands." In the apostle John's vision of the final revelation of Jesus Christ, God's blessing comes to those who die in the Lord, as the Spirit says, "that they may rest from their labors, for their deeds follow them!" (Rev. 14:13). Here is the sabbatical fulfillment of God's one creational purpose. What we do in the Lord, by the power of His Spirit, in politics and in every other earthly occupation will be brought to perfection in the final sabbath. We can be confident that our deeds of justice now are kingdom deeds that will never be lost. Christ is gathering them up into His great storehouse of treasures. They are gold that will not be destroyed by the fire because they are fruits of God's redeeming work in us.

Of all those who live on earth, we are most fortunate and have the most for which to be thankful. God has given us all things in the creation to enjoy and to nurture. We belong here. We were made for the earth and it for us. We have been called to be homesteaders and political creatures as the revealers of God in this age. And at the same time God is calling us to the greatest day of celebration that we can imagine—to God's own sabbath rest when all of His glory will be unveiled. That day is not of our making, but it is not another world. It will be the completion, the culmination of all our work on the earth. We are sojourners on the move toward the final revelation of justice and peace. The totality of our earhtly lives and service can and should be caught up in the expectancy of the coming kingdom. Christ the King is leading us toward fulfillment by directing our present steps carefully through the present age of earthly stewardship in all of life. Contemporary politics is an expectant calling in Christ for those who are His.

Also by the APJ Education Fund:

Christians Organizing for Political Service by James W. Skillen. A study guide based on the work of the Association for Public Justice.
ISBN: 0-936456-01-9